LOST BODIES

LOST BODIES

A CHRONICLE OF DEATHS, DISAPPEARANCES, AND DISCOVERIES

CHARTWELL
BOOKS

Quarto is the authority on a wide range of topics.

Quarto educates, entertains and enriches the lives of our readers—enthusiasts and lovers of hands-on living.

www.quartoknows.com

© 2017 Text & design JMS Books LLP

This edition published in 2017 by
Chartwell Books
an imprint of Book Sales
a division of Quarto Publishing Group USA Inc.
142 West 36th Street, 4th Floor
New York, New York 10018
USA

ISBN-13: 978-0-7858-3447-2

Designed by cbdesign

10 9 8 7 6 5 4 3 2 1

Printed in China

FSC

www.fsc.org

MIX
Paper from
responsible sources
FSC® C016973

CONTENTS

INTRODUCTION

In an ideal world, every single person would be born into a stable, uncomplicated society, live an exemplary life, die a natural death, and be laid to rest in peace for eternity in whatever manner accords with local customs. There would be no jealousies, no dynastic quarrels, no skulduggery; no murders, no intrigues, no mysterious disappearances. In fact, the word "history" would have no place in any language.

B UT WE DO NOT LIVE in such a world. Instead, the story of human evolution is awash with characters who are cunning, ambitious, and quite often wicked; and others who are creative, daring or innovative, or outstanding leaders. And what is remarkable is that the actions of one person in a short (sometimes extremely short) lifetime can have an impact, positive or negative, that lasts hundreds, even thousands of years—and we, in the twenty-first century, want to know where those people are, so we can remember them, or revere them, or, in some instances, even just be certain that they are in a place where they can no longer cause mayhem. We want to be able to visit their final resting place, and in most cases, we can.

But what of the handful of famous, or infamous, characters whose resting place, for one reason or another, was or still is "lost"? What of the two outstanding leaders, the Macedonian conqueror Alexander the Great and the English king Alfred the Great, whose respective remains are buried somewhere in Egypt and somewhere in the city of Winchester, England, but no one knows exactly where? What of the "bad guys" who are remembered for their cruelty— the Mongol despot Genghis Khan, possibly the cruelest man who ever lived, and Vlad III, ruler of Walachia, known as "the Impaler" to reflect his favored method of torture? They are both lost.

LOST OR "DISAPPEARED"?

What of the pioneering American aviator Amelia Earhart, the Norwegian explorer Roald Amundsen, the great wartime entertainer Glenn Miller, and the much-loved French writer Antoine de Saint-Exupéry, who all vanished while on a flight over water? What is their story? What of those whose remains were at one time conveniently misplaced or "disappeared" so that their graves would not become a shrine, such as the Argentine First Lady Eva Perón, the Cuban revolutionary Che Guevara, and the entire Russian royal family, the Romanovs? Those who were subjected to bizarre treatment after death, such as the ninth-century pope Formosus, the French "Good King" Henri IV, and the English Lord Protector Oliver Cromwell? And those who opted to lose themselves, such as the German dictator Adolf Hitler, the British aristocrat Lord Lucan, and (possibly) the Australian prime minister, Harold Holt?

These questions, and more, are addressed—and sometimes answered—in *Lost Bodies*. The book is divided into three chapters: Well and Truly Lost, for the remains of those characters in history whose whereabouts were once known but now are not (although we offer some ideas); Lost and Found, for those whose remains were more mislaid than lost and are now settled in what *should* be their final resting place; and Lost for Good, for those people who completely disappeared, sometimes leaving a tantalizing shred of evidence but, in the main, vanishing without trace so that we can only put forward theories about what happened to them and where they ended up.

Each story is set in its historical context, and includes not only a biography of the lost body concerned but also an explanation of the character's place in the social and political world of the time. Where there are intrigues and conspiracy theories, we share them—for example, did the English king Richard III (recently discovered with enormous public interest and reinterred with great ceremony) really dispose of his young and innocent nephews, "the Princes in the Tower," or was he simply a convenient peg on which to hang the label of "murderer"? Was Hitler's equally wicked sidekick, Martin Bormann, executed, did he commit suicide, or did he escape and live out his days in South America? And did Thomas Edison have a hand in the mysterious disappearance of his rival, the French-born inventor and cinema pioneer Louis Le Prince?

The contributors to *Lost Bodies* have brought you the most up-to-date information at the time of publication, but research into some of the cases is ongoing, so the stories may not have ended quite yet . . .

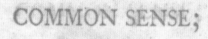

COMMON SENSE;

ADDRESSED TO THE

INHABITANTS

OF

AMERICA,

On the following interesting

SUBJECTS.

I. Of the Origin and Design of Government in general,
with concise Remarks on the English Constitution.

II. Of Monarchy and Hereditary Succession.

III. Thoughts on the present State of American Affairs.

IV. Of the present Ability of America, with some miscellaneous Reflections.

Man knows no Master save creating HEAVEN,
Or those whom choice and common good ordain.

THOMSON.

PHIA;

RELL, in Third-Street.

EXTRA THE STARS AND STRIPES EXTRA

HITLER DEAD

Fuehrer Fell at CP, German Radio Says;
Doenitz at Helm, Vows War Will Continue

Churchill
Hints Peace
Is at Hand

WELL AND TRULY LOST

With hundreds if not thousands of years having elapsed since the death and burial of significant historical figures, it is not surprising that their graves may have been lost. Natural disasters take place, countries are invaded, graves are ransacked, burial grounds are built over, and time marches on—leaving only rumors and trails gone cold in their place. Alexander the Great's tomb disappeared as long ago as the fourth century CE; and while the efforts made in Ancient Egypt to erase all traces of Queen Nefertiti may have been successful, they haven't deterred the archaeologists who continue to search for her. There is no grave at which to mourn more recent figures such as Thomas Paine and Davy Crockett, although the lack of a tomb might be just as well for figures as reviled as Vlad, "the Impaler," and Adolf Hitler. This chapter explores the cold cases of history—those still filed under "unsolved."

NEFERTITI

More than three thousand years ago Egypt was ruled by a glamorous and controversial power couple: Nefertiti and Akhenaten (formerly known as Amenhotep IV), the ninth pharaoh of the Eighteenth Dynasty. The name Nefertiti translates as "a beautiful woman has come," and among her many titles were "Lady of All Women," "Main King's Wife," "Great of Praises," and "Mistress of Upper and Lower Egypt."

Neferneferuaten-Nefertiti
Born: c. 1370 BCE
Spouse: Akhenaten
Children: Meritaten, Meketaten, Ankhesenpaaten, Nefernefeuaten Tasherit, Neferneferure, Setepenre
Ruled: c. 1353–1336 BCE
Died: c. 1330 BCE

BUT WHERE is the body of this queen, goddess, high priest at ceremonies, mother of six (some think seven), and wielder of enormous power? Her bust, housed in Berlin's Neues Museum, with its chiseled jawline, lean cheeks, and swanlike neck, is one of the most iconic symbols of Egypt, but rather like the *Mona Lisa*, Nefertiti remains an enigma portrayed in a beautiful work of art. She lived in extraordinary splendor but whether she was buried in similar circumstances remains a mystery.

PARENTS AND CHILDREN

Nefertiti's parentage is uncertain. She was not a royal but may have been the daughter of a high-ranking courtier called Aye and his wife Tey. It is thought she was chosen to marry Amenhotep at the age of 15, or possibly younger. The couple ruled together during the Eighteenth Dynasty from c. 1353 to 1336 BCE, with Nefertiti as chief consort and principal (but not only) wife. By the age of thirty, she had borne six daughters. There was also speculation that she was either the step-mother or even the mother of Tutankhamun, whom her daughter Ankhesenpaaten eventually married and who became the celebrated boy-king.

THE ATEN

The Egyptian court was a highly sophisticated place and the people submitted to their mighty ruler, who was protected by an elite team of bodyguards, some of whom were recruited from foreign lands. Nefertiti and Akhenaten's kingdom stretched from Nubia to Syria and they reigned during a period of enormous wealth, experiencing huge changes in art, society, and religion. Akhenaten abolished the traditional polytheistic religion, under which the priests enjoyed greater wealth and power than the pharaohs, closing their temples, erasing all signs of the pantheon, and imposing a new one-god state religion based

Iconic beauty. *The bust of Queen Nefertiti was found in 1912 at the archaelogical site of Amarna.*

A blessing from above. *Akhenaten, Nefertiti, and their children are blessed by the Aten.*

on the worship of the sun god, the Aten. The Aten was depicted as a sun disk with rays of light emanating from it, each one ending in a tiny human hand. The Aten's blessing was reserved for the king and queen alone, who were divine intermediaries and worshipped as such. Nefertiti took on the name of Neferneferuaten-Nefertiti ("the Aten is radiant of radiance because the Beautiful One has arrived") and was permitted by her husband to play a key role in the new religion, assuming the status of semidivine human being. Changing his name from Amenhotep to Akhenaten ("one who is effective for the Aten"), the pharaoh moved the capital from Thebes north to a virgin site that straddled the Nile. A new and extensive city called Akhetaten, now known as Armana, was constructed as a vast temple to Aten, adorned with carvings of the god and the royal couple. Nefertiti and Akhenaten were seen as joint rulers on Earth. The architect and ruler of this new city may have been viewed in his time as a despot, but historians describe Akhenaten as the first "individual" in human history thanks to his radical changes, and a prophet of arguably the world's first monotheistic religion. A royal tomb no doubt intended for the entire royal family was carved in a large wadi to the east of the city, but within just thirty years of its construction, the city, home to up to fifty thousand people at its height, had been abandoned.

"A beautiful thing is never perfect." —*Egyptian proverb*

DEATH AND DISAPPEARANCE

Everything changed in the twelfth year of Akhenaten's seventeen-year rule, with the deaths in quick succession of his second eldest daughter, Meketaten, his secondary wife Kiya, and his mother Tiy. Other daughters also disappeared from the records at the same time, followed by Nefertiti herself. Perhaps she fell out of favor (although an inscription dated to shortly before her husband's death describes her as his chief wife). Perhaps she succumbed to the plague or, as some have speculated, she became co-regent with her husband, possibly dressing as a man. Is Nefertiti in fact Neferneferuaten, the named co-regent?

Mummification

The Egyptians embalmed and preserved their dead in the belief that the body would be required in the afterlife. Through a process known as mummification, all moisture was removed, leaving a dried body that could resist decay. A hammer would be used to break the nose and a hook inserted to drain the brain. An incision would be made on the left side of the body to remove all internal organs, except for the heart, considered the center or seat of a person. The organs were dried and buried alongside the body, the cavity of which was filled with straw soaked in incense and resins, after which layers of bandages and linen shrouds were wrapped around the body.

Some scholars believe she may even have been Pharaoh Smenkhkare, who briefly ruled Egypt after Akhenaten's death before Tutankhamun came to power.

Akhenaten died in 1336 BCE and was laid to rest in a royal tomb with the image of Nefertiti depicted on all four corners of his sarcophagus. Turbulence ruled in both court and country and a marriage was arranged between 9-year old Tutankhaten, renamed Tutankhamun, and Nefertiti's third daughter Ankhesenpaaten, renamed Ankhesenamun, aged around 13. During the boy-king's brief reign the country turned full circle. The court returned to its traditional home, polytheism was reintroduced, and the supremacy of Amun was restored. But the beautiful queen, and all records of her, disappeared without trace. Why was such a powerful figure so comprehensively erased? Was it the work of those priests who had suffered under her and her husband's rule?

A display of power. *Queen Nefertiti performs a royal ceremony in an illustration by Fortunino Matania (1927).*

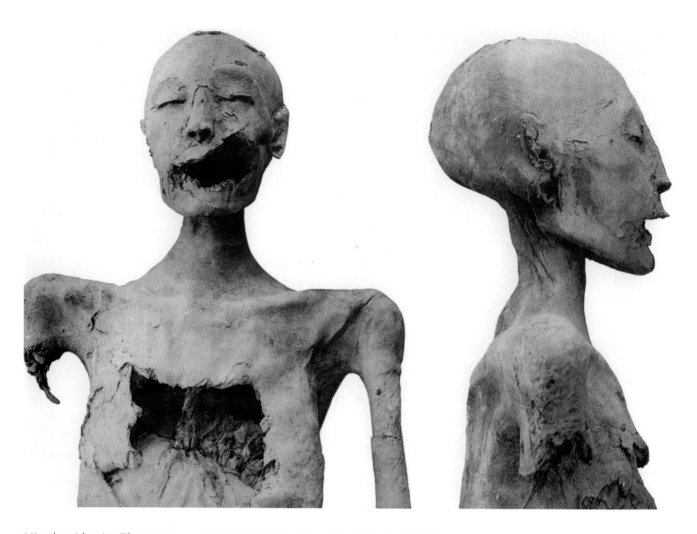

Mistaken identity. *The mummy of the "Younger Lady," once believed to be Nefertiti but now thought to be the mother of Tutankhamun.*

NEFERTITI COMES TO LIGHT

Nefertiti's beautiful face emerged from the darkness into the light again in 1912 with the discovery of her bust. The iconic painted limestone sculpture was dated to 1345 BCE and was found in a sculptor's workshop in Armana.

In 1898, three unidentified mummies, partially destroyed by looters, were discovered in the Valley of the Kings, near modern-day Luxor (the site of ancient Thebes), in a side room of the tomb of Amenhotep III, Akhenaten's father. The mummies were of two women and a boy, and one of the women, known as the "Younger Lady," had a shaven head and wig (a sign that the owner was a woman of power). Remnants of the wig were taken to Cairo museum after the bodies were photographed and resealed. In 2003, Dr Joann Fletcher, a British Egyptologist and author of the book *The Search for Nefertiti*, published the following year, examined the wig and studied the photographs of the resealed mummies. She hypothesized, controversially, that this could be the body of Nefertiti, suggesting that the wig matched the Nubian-style hairpieces worn by the queen and her court. During lengthy research, Dr Fletcher suggested that other findings could indicate a royal status, including a double piercing on one ear—a rare practice attributed to the court of Nefertiti—and the impression of a tight band on the forehead. Could these be the bodies of Nefertiti, Akhenaten's

"To speak the name of the dead is to make them live again." —*Egyptian tomb inscription*

mother, and one of his brothers? The findings were challenged and dismissed by some.

SEARCH FOR THE MUMMY

Repeated attempts have been made to identify a number of mummies as that of Nefertiti. Excavations in and around Egypt's Valley of the Kings have revealed many tombs and attached chambers. In 2015, British Egyptologist Nicholas Reeves argued in a provocative paper called "The Burial of Nefertiti?," published by the Armana Royal Tombs Project, that her body could have been placed in a mausoleum befitting her status that was subsequently also used for Tutankhamun upon his unexpected and early demise. His suggestion that she could lie buried behind ghost doors leading to a chamber behind the north wall of the tomb so famously discovered by Howard Carter in 1922 is based on laser scans that mapped out King Tut's burial chamber. If Nefertiti had ruled alongside him, it would make sense for them to be buried within the same grave complex. Further scans have been performed that challenge the theory of the presence of hidden chambers but the results remain unpublished and uncertain in a difficult local political climate.

Some scholars have suggested that she could have been his mother, but DNA tests in 2010 support claims that his father was Akhenaten and his mother was Akhenaten's unnamed sister, the mummy now known as "Younger Lady."

The search for this enigmatic, beautiful woman continues. If her body is discovered, it will be a sensational find, but perhaps some of the fascination about Nefertiti lies in the very fact that she eludes discovery. There is also the possibility that her mummy simply did not survive and will therefore never be found. And even if positive identification is made, might it not be better to leave her remains safely where they are? In the meantime, the search—and the mystery—continue.

Egyptian botox
Scientists from the Image Science Institute in Berlin, Germany, have analyzed the bust of Nefertiti and discovered evidence that her beauty may have been enhanced with a bump on her nose smoothed out, creases around her mouth and cheeks erased, and more prominence given to her cheekbones. These changes may have been made to make the queen's features more in line with ideals of beauty at the time.

Buried secrets in King Tut's chamber? *British archaeologist Nicholas Reeves and Egyptian minister of antiquities, Mamdouh Eldamaty, in the Valley of the Kings in Luxor, Egypt.*

ANTONY AND CLEOPATRA

"She came sailing up the river Cydnus, in a barge with gilded stern and outspread sails of purple, while oars of silver beat time to the music of flutes and fifes and harps. She herself lay all along under a canopy of cloth of gold, dressed as Venus in a picture, and beautiful young boys, like painted Cupids, stood on each side to fan her." So Plutarch described Cleopatra's glittering arrival in the life of Mark Antony and the moment their lives converged forever.

CLEOPATRA, RULER OF EGYPT and one of the most celebrated women in history, was not Egyptian but a member of the Macedonian Greek dynasty that had ruled the ancient land since the time of Alexander the Great. In 51 BCE, aged 18, she became pharaoh on the death of her father Ptolemy XII, ruling jointly with her younger brother Ptolemy XIII.

THE SEDUCTION OF CAESAR

Cleopatra proved her mettle early on. In around 48 BCE, when relations with her brother and his advisors broke down, she left Alexandria to go into exile but promptly raised an army in Arab lands in order to fight back. It was at this point that Julius Caesar arrived in Egypt, in pursuit of fellow Roman statesman Pompey with whom he was at war, only to find on arrival that Pompey was already dead— killed on the orders of Cleopatra's brother, who hoped to curry favor with Caesar. Caesar professed horror at the murder of a man who, although his rival, was a senator, and refused to look at the severed head presented to him.

The scene was now set for the first of the legendary parts of the story: Realizing her brother would want to get Caesar, who had by now installed himself in the palace at Alexandria, and the might of Rome on his side, 21-year-old Cleopatra had a trick up her sleeve. She concealed herself in a rug and had herself carried through the palace to be unrolled with a flourish in front of the 52-year-old general—some sources say it is more likely that she was hidden in a bag used for carrying laundry, tied at the top in order to drop down seductively over

Cleopatra VII Thea Philopator
Born: *c.* 69 BCE Alexandria (?)
Spouse: Ptolemy XIV
Children: Ptolemy XV Caesar ("Caesarion," 47 BCE), Alexander Helios and Cleopatra Selene (40 BCE), Ptolemy Philadelphus (36 BCE)
Died: 30 BCE, Alexandria

Marcus Antonius (Mark Antony)
Born: 83 BCE, Rome
Spouse: Fadia (?); Antonia Hybrida Minor (?); Fulvia (m. 44 BCE); Octavia Minor (m. 40 BCE)
Children: Antonia Prima (50 BCE), Marcus Antonius Antyllus (47 BCE), Iullus Antonius (45 BCE), Alexander Helios and Cleopatra Selene (40 BCE), Antonia Major (39 BCE), Antonia Minor (36 BCE), Ptolemy Philadelphus (36 BCE)
Died: 30 BCE, Alexandria

In Shakespeare's words. *In his version of the famous love affair, Shakespeare has Antony reveal his infatuation with eloquence, "My heart was to thy rudder tied by the strings," Antony and Cleopatra, Act III, Scene XI.*

True likenesses? Busts said to be of Cleopatra and Mark Antony, although the only certain known images of them are on coins. However, these busts do show Cleopatra with a prominent nose, while they give Antony a jutting chin and a broken nose but still a fine head of hair.

her shoulders for that important "ta dah" first impression. Whatever method was used, the ruse worked. That night they became lovers.

Once it was clear that Caesar favored Cleopatra over her brother, Ptolemy challenged Caesar and war broke out, culminating in the Battle of the Nile. Ptolemy drowned and Caesar was victorious, restoring Cleopatra to the throne in 47 BCE along with her next surviving brother, Ptolemy XIV. They probably ruled jointly in name only—with Cleopatra being in real control, despite taking "keep it in the family" to the extreme by marrying him as tradition dictated. Shortly afterward, probably still in 47 BCE, Cleopatra gave birth to a child she named Ptolemy XV Caesar, also known as Caesarion or "little Caesar." It is not clear whether Caesar senior actually acknowledged him as his son, but it is generally thought that he was Caesar's child and Cleopatra named the infant as her heir.

Caesar returned to Rome, but was assassinated on March 15, 44 BCE. Back in Alexandria Ptolemy XIV, too, died, possibly poisoned on Cleopatra's orders. Whatever the case, Cleopatra now ruled Egypt with her son, a situation soon to be disrupted by the arrival of Mark Antony.

MARK ANTONY

Mark Antony was a Roman statesman and military commander, serving initially in Syria and Egypt and then joining Julius Caesar's campaign in Gaul (present-day France). He supported Caesar (to whom he was distantly related) when civil war broke out between Caesar and Pompey in 49 BCE, and in 45 BCE he was elected consul, serving alongside Caesar, but the following year Caesar was assassinated. Antony spoke at Caesar's funeral, using his eulogy to stoke the ill feeling toward his assassins—who believed they had liberated Rome from a dictator—into downright anger. The killers, including the chief conspirators Cassius and Brutus, were obliged to flee Rome.

Named in Caesar's will as his heir, Caesar's 18-year-old great-nephew Octavian now arrived in Italy, but there was discord with Antony almost immediately—the details of Caesar's will became a source of conflict and Octavian represented a challenge to Antony's authority as consul. However, in 43 BCE an alliance was agreed between the pair and they formed the Second Triumverate, along with Lepidus, another military commander and supporter of Caesar. The pact awarded the trio joint power over the Roman empire and divided it up between them—Octavian ruling the West, Lepidus Africa, and Antony the eastern provinces.

THEIR PATHS COINCIDE

One of Antony's first actions as triumvir was to order Cleopatra to appear before him at Tarsus (in present-day Turkey), to explain her actions after Caesar's assassination. The charge was that she had given aid to the assassins, although it may have been a pretext to obtain Egyptian support for Antony's military campaigns. But Cleopatra was not one to trot along meekly at Antony's summons. She dallied and arrived late by barge, although the word "barge" hardly does justice to the sheer magnificence of the spectacle that greeted the Roman general when she arrived. "The word went through all the multitude, that Venus was come to feast with Bacchus," wrote first-century Greek historian Plutarch.

Evidently this had considerable effect because Cleopatra now took her second Roman lover and, instead of taking care of business and returning to the capital, where Octavian's power was growing meanwhile, Antony spent the next few

The Meeting of Antony and Cleopatra. *As imagined by Sir Lawrence Alma-Tadema in 1882. "She herself lay all along under a canopy of cloth of gold, dressed as Venus in a picture." Plutarch.*

The Temple of Dendera. *Located 35 miles/56 kilometers north of Luxor, the temple wall depicts Cleopatra (shown on the left) making offerings to the gods.*

months in Egypt, before eventually returning to Italy in spring 40 BCE. Shortly after, Cleopatra gave birth to Antony's twins, named Alexander and Cleopatra, but did not meet him again for another three years. When his wife Fulvia died later in 40 BCE, Antony—despite his liaison with Cleopatra—married Octavian's sister Octavia in a bid to ease the tension between the two men. But in 37 BCE Cleopatra, joined Antony in Antioch and later gave birth to another child of his, a boy she named Ptolemy Philadelphus. And on his return from a disastrous campaign in Parthia (part of present-day Iran), Antony avoided Octavia, instead heading straight for Alexandria and Cleopatra. It is not clear if he ever married Cleopatra, but it would have been illegal according to Roman law.

THE ROT SETS IN

In 34 BCE the antagonism between Antony and Octavian and the Roman Senate was brought to a head with an event that came to be known as the "Donations of Alexandria," when Antony assigned a number of territories held by him in the name of Rome to Cleopatra and her children. He also pronounced Caesarion joint ruler of Egypt with Cleopatra, and divorced Octavia. This provoked great anger in the Roman Senate, where Octavian fanned the flames by reading out a document that he claimed was Antony's will. In it Antony supposedly recognized Caesarion as Caesar's heir and gave further legacies to his children with Cleopatra. And to add insult to injury, he gave instructions that he should be buried in Alexandria beside Cleopatra, not in Rome. With rumors circulating that Antony also planned to transfer the capital from Rome to Alexandria, it must have seemed that a powerful empire was now developing on the doorstep of the Roman state.

Egyptian queen seeks Roman general for loving relationship—the myth meets the (possible) truth

Antony: *Able and accomplished statesman and military leader, enjoys the good life. Strong and handsome physique.* Antony was born into an impoverished but noble family. He was genial and generous and loved by his men, and would eat with them "off the common soldiers' tables."

Cleopatra: *Witty and sophisticated, with striking looks. Intelligent and astute. Fluent Egyptian and knowledge of several other languages.* Much has been written about Cleopatra's appearance—was she a ravishing siren, or plain or even ugly? Some coins and busts depict her with a prominent, slightly hooked nose. Despite her liaisons with Caesar and Antony, it is unlikely that she had a string of lovers, contrary to her portrayal in history. There was almost certainly a degree of expediency involved with her affairs—no doubt mutual, who could be useful to whom—but it seems that, at least in the case of Antony, genuine attraction developed into real love.

However, instead of declaring war on Antony, which would have alienated those factions still supporting him, Octavian and the Senate set their sights on Cleopatra.

The Egyptian and Roman forces clashed at the Battle of Actium, fought in the waters off Greece, on September 2, 31 BCE. The battle was a disaster for Antony. Octavian's general Agrippa outmaneuvered him and his troops started to defect to Agrippa, perhaps seeing the writing on the wall. Over the months that followed Antony fought a series of small skirmishes with Octavian until finally what was left of Antony's defeated forces deserted him.

DOUBLE SUICIDE

Now comes the second momentous part of the tale, in a story already stuffed with legend. Again the details are sketchy in the extreme but the most usual version of events is that after the defeat, fearing capture by Octavian, Cleopatra retreated to her mausoleum. Antony received the news—which turned out to be false—that Cleopatra had committed suicide, and so fell on his sword in true Roman style on August 1, 30 BCE. But he did not die immediately and when he learned that Cleopatra was still alive, asked to be taken to her. Since the heavy doors to the mausoleum were shut, he was hoisted in through a window and died in her arms. Octavian allowed Cleopatra to attend to his funeral arrangements. Just a few days later, on August 10, after bathing and dressing in her finery, the Egyptian queen ate a last meal and then took her own life. If some historians and a thousand popular images are to be believed, the method she chose was by holding a poisonous snake—an asp—to her bosom. But even Greek historian Plutarch admitted, writing just a few decades later, "The truth of the matter no one knows." Antony and Cleopatra had been together, on and off, for eleven years.

> "She shall be buried by her Antony / No grave upon the earth shall clip in it / A pair so famous." —Antony and Cleopatra, *William Shakespeare*

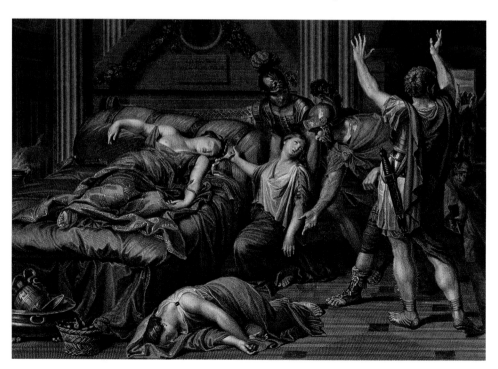

The death of Cleopatra.
Possibly the most famous deathbed scene in history.

The search continues. *Fragments of bone, Taposiris Magna (above), one of the sites believed to contain the remains of Cleopatra. A sphinx (below), believed to represent Cleopatra's father Ptolemy XII, discovered during excavations of the ancient harbor of Alexandria.*

WHERE ARE THEY NOW?

It was said that, honoring Cleopatra's wish, Octavian had her buried beside Antony in Alexandria, but the tomb has been lost for centuries. Recent attempts to find it have focused on two locations. In 1992, a team from the IEASM (European Institute for Underwater Archaeology) led by Franck Goddio and in cooperation with the Egyptian Supreme Council of Antiquities began exploring the site of ancient Alexandria, which now lies beneath the waves—a combination of earthquakes, tidal waves, and subsidence saw to it that by the eighth century CE the royal palaces had disappeared from view. Although they were not specifically searching for evidence of Cleopatra, during the excavations divers found coins bearing the queen's likeness. Some years later, in 2009, Greek marine archaeologists discovered a large block of granite that could have formed the threshold for a monumental door around 23 feet/7 meters high. Could it be the entrance to Cleopatra's mausoleum? It seems entirely plausible that she and Antony would have been buried together there.

The second location is a temple dedicated to the gods Isis and Osiris at Taposiris Magna, about 30 miles/50 kilometers west of Alexandria. A team led by Egyptologist Dr Zahi Hawass found twenty-seven tombs, including ten mummies, which it appears had been buried with their faces turned toward the temple, indicating the presence of a significant burial.

Dr Kathleen Martinez Berry, criminal lawyer turned archaeologist, is convinced that the tomb lies here. A huge underground necropolis was discovered close to the temple containing eight hundred skeletons, including some with skulls gilded with gold, along with coins bearing the image of Cleopatra and many other artifacts from her time. The many significant finds indicate that the temple site was extremely important. This coupled with the fact that Cleopatra styled herself a "new Isis" would seem to back up Berry's instincts. Everything seems to point toward the presence of a high-status individual at the site— but where? Excavations are ongoing.

ALEXANDER THE GREAT

Alexander III, dubbed "the Great," ruled for just thirteen years. And yet in that short time he conquered much of the known world of his day, without losing a single battle, and inspired the renowned Hellenistic period of culture and art. His remarkable legacy survives, but his tomb is lost—although there have been nearly one hundred and fifty officially recognized attempts to locate it.

Alexander III
Born: July 356 BCE, Pella, Macedonia
Spouse: Roxana (m. 327–323 BCE); Stateira II (m. 324–323 BCE); Parysatis (m. 324–323 BCE)
Children: Heracles of Macedon (b. 327 BCE); Alexander IV of Macedon (b. 323 Alexandria, Egypt)
Died: June 323 BCE, Babylon (in present-day Iraq)
Buried: Alexandria, Egypt

ALEXANDER'S PARENTS were Philip II, of the Ancient Greek kingdom of Macedon, and Olympias of Epirus, one of Philip's seven (or thereabouts) wives. The Greek historian Diodorus Siculus described Philip as a king who "stands out above all others for his military acumen, personal courage, and intellectual brilliance." He could equally have been describing Alexander.

A QUESTION OF LEGITIMACY

Philip II ascended the throne of Macedon, located to the north-east of Greece, in 359 BCE. His was a modest kingdom, but he was ambitious; he created a disciplined army of infantry wielding sarissas—double-pointed pikes—up to 20 feet/6 meters long, organized them into a complex and tactically brilliant battle formation known as the Macedonian phalanx, and systematically conquered all the major Greek city-states.

Meanwhile, Olympias was as ambitious for their son as Philip was for himself, and with her encouragement the king was grooming Alexander as heir to the Macedonian throne. Philip valued culture and education, so Alexander was taught how to read, write, and play the lyre. Later, Philip engaged the famous Greek philosopher Aristotle as a private tutor for Alexander, a relationship that helped shape the boy's character. Alexander also learned everything he would need in order to be an effective military leader—how to march, fight, and ride. At the age of around 12, he tamed Bucephalus, a beautiful but wild black stallion, a feat that has now passed into legend. Watching others attempting to approach him, Alexander observed that the horse was afraid of his own shadow, and calmed him by turning him away from the sun so that his shadow was behind him.

Victorious war hero. A *marble bust of Alexander made in the eponymous city of Alexandria, Egypt, c. 200 BCE. The leonine mane of hair hints at his power.*

Despite all this, Philip's nobles eyed Alexander with suspicion, considering him a half-breed (Olympias's father was king of a neighboring realm), and when Philip took a new wife, a Macedonian, Alexander's legitimacy was called into question—in Philip's eyes, as well as his court's. By now, Alexander was in his late teens, quite old enough to become his father's enemy, and there is speculation that when Philip was assassinated by his own bodyguard in 336 BCE, Alexander and his mother were behind it. Whether that is true or not, Philip's Macedonian wife had not produced an alternative heir and Alexander inherited the title. He recognized that his claim would be unpopular, and took steps to establish his effectiveness as a military commander. But first he took a few precautions—he honored his father with an extravagant funeral and an elaborate tomb, then, with the help of his mother, bumped off a few potential rivals.

A MILITARY GENIUS

Having removed any obstacles in his path, Alexander launched his military campaign—and succeeded in dramatic style. What his father had begun, Alexander took to a new level between 334 and 324 BCE, utilizing Philip's Macedonian phalanx to great effect and quickly gaining a reputation for speed and efficiency in battle. His immediate aim was to topple Darius III, king of the vast Achaemenid Empire of Persia, which stretched from Egypt across western Asia to northern India and central Asia. Darius was no match for Alexander's might in combat, and was soundly defeated by him at their final meeting, the Battle of Gaugamela, in 331 BCE; however, when Darius met his death the following year it was at the hand of a traitorous cousin. Alexander promptly assumed leadership of the empire, including Egypt, which had been under Persian occupation for nearly two centuries and welcomed him as a liberator.

Aged only 25, Alexander was the "great king" of Persia, and he proceeded to create a huge network of trade and commerce, ingratiating himself with his ethnically diverse range of subjects by adopting their customs, even to the extent of dressing in

Conqueror of Persia. The Alexander Mosaic, *dating from the third century* BCE, *was discovered in the ruins of Pompeii in 1831. It depicts a battle between Alexander and the Persian king Darius III.*

the style of Persian royalty. He founded more than 70 new cities, naming them all Alexandria, including one with the suffix Bucephala in memory of his beloved horse, fatally wounded in battle on the site in 326 BCE.

In 327 BCE Alexander recruited thirty thousand Persian soldiers into his army, known as the "successors," to safeguard the future of his empire, and in 324 BCE he organized a mass wedding in the Persian city of Susa, taking a Persian wife for himself—a daughter of Darius—and arranging marriages to noble Persian wives for his officers. The wedding was not a sentimental gesture, but the symbolic union of the Persian and Macedonian cultures.

DEATH OF THE GREAT ALEXANDER

In 323 BCE, Alexander was hosting a feast in Babylon, on the bank of the Euphrates, when he collapsed in great pain. The source of his agony was never established, although poisoning by a rival was not ruled out as a possibility. Diseases such as malaria, meningitis, or typhoid have also been mooted as a potential cause, or even raising his glass in one toast too many (his tendency to drink to excess was well-known). Whatever the cause, he suffered ten days of high fever, and died soon afterward. Alexander the Great's reign was over and his ambition to expand his empire still farther died with him.

A horse fit for a general. Alexander Taming Bucephalus, *by the French artist François Schommer, depicts Alexander turning the horse's head away from the sun so it would no longer fear its own shadow.*

ALEXANDER'S LEGACY

Alexander left a vast empire but no legitimate heir to control it, and instead nominated his four strongest generals, known as the Diadochi: Cassander, Ptolemy, Antigonus, and Seleucus. After Alexander's death, the generals, his court, and his family entered into a battle of their own over the succession. Cassander—a Macedonian noble and possible candidate for Alexander's assassin (if indeed he was assassinated)—executed Olympias and anyone else he deemed a troublesome obstacle, including Alexander's favorite wife, Roxana, and his posthumously born son, Alexander IV. Cassander went on to rule the kingdom of Macedonia and the rest of the empire was divided into individual kingdoms under rulers who simply were not in Alexander's league.

But Alexander left much more than chaos behind him. He initiated the Hellenistic World, spreading Greek culture, language, art, and philosophy throughout his empire. Following the example set by his tutor, Aristotle,

The Temple of Artemis
Alexander began his Persian Empire campaign with the liberation of Ephesus, an important trading port. Legend has it that the goddess Artemis was so focused on ensuring Alexander's safe arrival in the world that she failed to prevent her temple at Ephesus being destroyed by fire on the night of his birth. There was also said to be a bright star shining over Macedonia that night, an auspicious sign.

Alexander's funeral procession. *This nineteenth-century interpretation is based on a description by the Greek historian Diodorus of Sicily in his Bibliotheca historica.*

Alexander did not force this knowledge upon his subjects— he merely offered it. And it was a two-way process—Greek artistic style was enhanced by the exotic influences of the regions. Rome, too, fell under the spell, and interest in Greek art and culture continued throughout the Roman imperial period; but ironically Rome also brought an end to the Hellenistic dynasty, dated to the Battle of Actium in 31 BCE.

A SUCCESSION OF TOMBS

As to Alexander himself, his generals argued for two years over what to do with his body. Eventually, it was loaded onto a golden chariot—preserved in a sarcophagus full of honey, according to legend—and the funeral cortege set off to bury him in Macedon. However, it was highjacked en route by Alexander's friend and advisor Ptolemy, founder of the Egyptian Ptolemaic dynasty, who seized the corpse and buried it in a tomb in Memphis in lower Egypt. Some time later, it was reburied in Alexandria, the "Pearl of the Mediterranean" founded by Alexander in 331 BCE and expanded by Ptolemy to become the largest city in the known world at the time and a renowned seat of learning. No evidence of either of these tombs has ever been found. In the late third century BCE, Alexander was reburied yet again, this time in a communal mausoleum in Alexandria with all the deceased Ptolemaic rulers.

ALEXANDER RECEIVES VISITORS

Records show that Alexander's third tomb was visited by some of the most well-known figures in history—among them Julius Caesar, Cleopatra, Hadrian, and Augustus. According to Suetonius, in his *Life of Augustus*, the founder of the Roman Empire "honored him [Alexander] with a golden crown which he placed on his head and covered him with flowers …" He is also said to have bent to kiss the corpse and in so doing accidentally dislodged a bit of Alexander's mummified nose. In 199 CE, the tomb was sealed by the Roman emperor Septimus Severus, and the last recorded visit was in 215 CE.

Several early Christian Church Fathers recorded that, by the fourth century CE, the location of the tomb was unknown; however, in later centuries, the Arab historian Al-Masudi and author Leo the African both reported visiting it. Neither of them thought to specify the location for the benefit of future seekers.

Hephaestion

Alexander's closest friend was his one-time lover, Hephaestion, who married Alexander's sister-in-law at Susa. Plutarch, the Greek biographer (46–*c*.119 CE), recorded that when Hephaestion died later that year of a mysterious ailment, Alexander had his doctor crucified, and for good measure massacred a whole tribe as offerings for Hephaestion's spirit.

ALEXANDER AND THE ORACLE OF AMUN

In 1989, a Greek archaeologist, Liana Souvaltzi, was convinced she had found Alexander's tomb—not in Alexandria at all, but near the oasis of Siwa in western Egypt. It is a location with a remarkable connection to Alexander, who claimed that his real father was Zeus, the supreme god in Greek mythology and the equivalent of the Egyptian god Amun Ra—a belief instilled by his mother. In 331 BCE, when Alexander was 25, he undertook the challenging journey to Siwa to consult the renowned Oracle of Amun. Speculation was rife as to the nature of the question Alexander put to the oracle—"Will I conquer the entire world?" was naturally a front-runner—but according to legend the oracle confirmed his divinity. Alexander expressed a wish to be buried at Siwa.

POLITICAL INTRIGUE

After initial excavations, Ms Souvaltzi and her team discovered an entrance guarded by lion statues, and further exploration revealed what appeared to be a large and magnificent Hellenistic royal tomb. There were more lion heads, indicating the elevated status of the tomb's occupant, as well as an eight-pointed star, the symbol of the Macedonian royal family. Three broken stone tablets bore inscriptions referring to Alexander—the largest of which, apparently composed by Ptolemy, was translated as "I ... carried the corpse here ... when I was commander of Egypt. It was I who was caring about his secrets, and who was carrying out his wishes ..." Surely, when the final burial chamber was opened, it would contain the mummified body of Alexander the Great?

But Souvaltzi's hopes for solving the mystery of Alexander's whereabouts were dashed when her excavation permit was suddenly withdrawn. Not only that, but a team of Greek government archaeologists visited the site and declared there was no evidence that the structure was even a tomb, let alone that of Alexander; that the structure was not in the Macedonian style; and that the fragments of stone tablets dated from the Roman period, long after Alexander's death.

Souvaltzi has stuck to her guns, however, and in 2014 reiterated her claim, insisting that her findings have been blocked as a result of diplomatic intervention by the Greek and Egyptian governments. The fact that the monument stands under constant guard would seem to suggest that she's absolutely right. But if the tomb does indeed contain Alexander's remains, as Souvaltzi passionately believes, then it begs a very pertinent question: Upon whom did Emperor Augustus bestow that respectful (and slightly destructive) kiss?

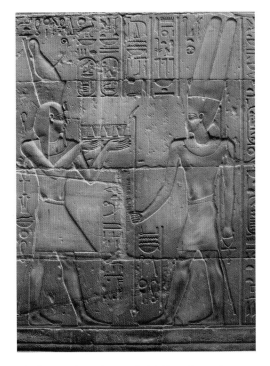

Egyptian god. An *Egyptian wall relief of Alexander in the Temple of Luxor. He was anointed as pharaoh in Memphis in 332* BCE, *having studied Egyptian laws and customs in preparation.*

Final resting place? An *archaeological site near the Siwa Oasis in Egypt's Western Desert, seat of the oracle temple of Amun. Greek archaeologist Liana Souvaltzi believes the site holds the tomb of Alexander the Great.*

ALFRED THE GREAT

The Anglo-Saxon king Alfred is the only English monarch to be dubbed "The Great." It is a tribute richly deserved; Alfred not only instigated a peace settlement that gave birth to the English nation, but also strived to share his love of learning with his people. He was buried in his capital, the city of Winchester—and reburied, and reburied …

Alfred
Born: 849, Wantage, England
Spouse: Ealhswith of Mercia
Children: Aelfthryth,
   Aethelflaed, Aethelgifu,
   Edward, Aethelweard
Died: 899, Winchester,
   England
Buried: Hyde Abbey,
   Winchester

NINTH-CENTURY ENGLAND was a collection of warring kingdoms, yet to be unified; Danish Viking raiders conquered the north and east of the country and in 871 set their sights on the south. King Aethelred of Wessex and his brother Alfred battled together to fend off the onslaught, but then Aethelred died, leaving 21-year-old Alfred to accede to the throne—and take on the Danes alone.

AT WAR WITH THE VIKINGS

The Vikings were pagan, and had no respect for Christianity, by now well established in Britain. Among their early victims were monastic communities on islands, most famously Lindisfarne, known as Holy Island and described by Northumbrian scholar Alcuin as "a place more sacred than any in Britain." Lindisfarne came under vicious attack in 793 and, before long, Vikings were not only raiding the country, but taking up residence; between 866 and 874, the Danish "Great Heathen Army" took control of the kingdoms of Northumbria, East Anglia, and Mercia. Wessex was now the last independent Anglo-Saxon kingdom—and the Danes' next target.

   In 871, shortly before his accession, Alfred had led his brother Aethelred's forces to defeat the Danes at the Battle of Ashdown. It was a short-lived and hard-won triumph. The Danes were undaunted; on January 6, 878, they captured Chippenham, a royal stronghold where Alfred was spending the winter with

The Vikings
"Viking" is an Old Norse word meaning "a pirate raid," and the marauding Vikings became known as the "raiders from the sea." According to records, they began their assault on Britain toward the end of the eighth century, and the sight of their distinctive longships, with fearsome carved dragon heads roaring from the bows, soon came to strike terror in the heart.

"The Great" monarch. A *nineteenth-century depiction of Alfred the Great with the trappings of power, after a painting, now lost, that hung in the Bodleian Library, Oxford University, England.*

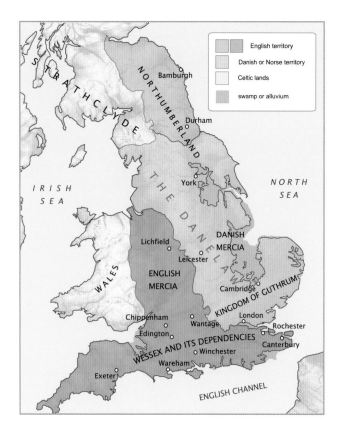

The extent of Danelaw.

A map of Britain at the time of the "Danelaw," showing the division of England between the English and the Vikings.

his family, and Saxon England was all but lost. Alfred retreated west and took refuge in the wild and inhospitable marshes of the Somerset Levels. Here he regrouped; he constructed a new stronghold on the island of Athelney, strengthening ancient defenses established in the Iron Age, and devised a strategy of guerrilla tactics.

Only a few months later, in May, Alfred defeated the Danes at the Battle of Edington, herded them back to Chippenham, and starved them until they surrendered. Under the terms of the surrender, Guthrum, the Danish leader, was obliged to convert to Christianity; he was baptized near Athelney, taking the name Aethelstan, with Alfred as his godfather. Alfred founded a Benedictine monastery on Athelney in 888, in thanks for his victory.

ALFRED BUILDS HIS DEFENSES

Alfred was under no illusion that his triumph at Edington would be the end of hostilities between the Anglo-Saxons and Vikings, and he began to restructure the defense of his kingdom against attack from both land and sea. He reorganized his militia into a standing defense force; he created a network of strategically spaced fortified settlements; and he founded the first English navy, equipped with large oared ships built to his own design, to patrol the coastline. His goal was not to prolong the conflict, however, but to unite England and bring about a lasting peace.

THE PEACE OF ALFRED AND GUTHRUM

When Guthrum attacked again in 884, Alfred defeated him. The outcome was a treaty that established a clear boundary dividing England into two. The area to the north and east, the "Danelaw," was subject to Scandinavian laws and customs, while the area to the south continued to be subject to Saxon laws and customs. It was a clever move on Alfred's part—by recognizing rather than repelling the Danish occupation, he set the stage for a united England, and he and his successors gradually reclaimed control of the whole country.

Alfred as statesman

It might seem that Alfred's entire reign was dominated by measures to deal with Viking invaders—indeed, they tried their luck again in the 890s and were thwarted by Alfred's defenses. However, Alfred was not only a great warrior but also a great statesman, and he used his skill to rebuild the Anglo-Saxon kingdom he loved and mourned. He introduced a new legal code based on elements from earlier legislation, with amendments and additions of his own. He reformed the coinage, imposing stricter controls on minting. Above all, he exercised his highly developed sense of justice, and was particularly protective of those who were weak and dependent.

ALFRED AND ENGLISHNESS

Alfred was educated, spiritual, and English through and through, and once he had resolved the Viking problem he poured his energies into reviving Anglo-Saxon culture and promoting literacy and creativity. Literary works were written in Latin, the universal language of learning, putting them beyond the reach of ordinary people; so Alfred translated the books "most necessary for all men to know," such as Bede's *Ecclesiastical History of the English Peoples*, into Anglo-Saxon. His legal code was written in Old English, as was the *Anglo-Saxon Chronicle*, a record of political, social, and economic events begun in 891.

> "He seems to me a very foolish man ... who will not increase his understanding while he is in the world." —*Alfred the Great*

Alfred was also a patron of traditional arts and crafts, and the latter years of his reign saw a revival in the production of exquisite gold and silver jewelry and illuminated manuscripts. By his death in 899, he had done everything possible to preserve his heritage and that of his people.

TWO MINSTERS ...

Winchester, the ancient capital of Wessex and later of all Saxon England, is Alfred's city. It became the royal and ecclesiastical center of Wessex in the 670s, when its minster church acquired cathedral status. This church is now referred to as the "Old Minster," and it was here that Alfred was buried in 899—but it was only ever intended as a temporary interment.

The Alfred Jewel. *Inscribed "Alfred had me made," this work of art was discovered in 1693 in a peat bog near Athelney in Somerset, England.*

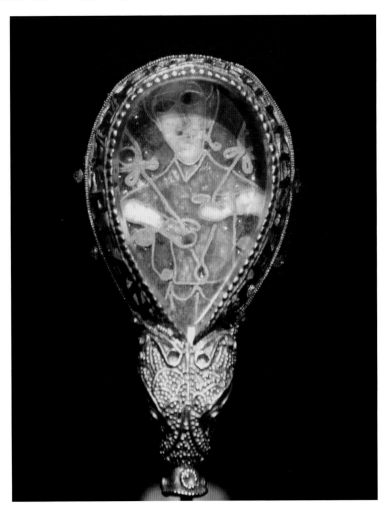

The descriptor "Old" implies that there is a "New," and this is indeed the case. Alfred had bought land adjacent to the old minster, intending to found a monastery, and after his death, his son and successor King Edward the Elder completed the project. The twelfth-century historian William of Malmesbury records that after Alfred's death, "the canons ... asserted that the royal spirit, resuming its carcass, wandered nightly through the buildings." However, once the new minster had been dedicated in 903, a solemn procession transferred Alfred's body to his permanent burial site, ensuring that he would now have "a quiet resting-place."

Alfred's widow, meanwhile, founded a convent, known as the Nunnaminster. There were now three religious foundations in close proximity, which, when the bishop's palace was added in the late tenth century and the New Minster extended to become one of the largest churches in England, formed a vast ecclesiastical complex. Alfred would have been delighted to know that it also became one of England's most important centers of learning and art.

A noble king. *This imposing bronze statue of* Alfred the Great *has guarded the English city of Winchester since 1901, the millenary of his death.*

... AND AN ABBEY

William the Conqueror arrived on England's shores in 1066 and within the space of a day Saxon rule was out and Norman rule was in, both royally and ecclesiastically. Winchester's New Minster was quickly replaced by an even larger, Romanesque-style cathedral, leaving the monks—together with Alfred and his family—in need of a new home. In 1110, Alfred's remains were once again the subject of a solemn procession, accompanied by treasures including the golden cross presented to New Minster by Canute, the Danish king of England who was to unite the realm, finishing what Alfred had begun. Alfred's destination this time was Hyde Abbey, just beyond the city walls, where he was reburied before the high altar of the abbey church.

DISSOLUTION OF THE MONASTERIES

It might reasonably be considered that this was at last Alfred's moment to settle once and for all, and indeed it might have been, had it not been for King Henry VIII's all-consuming desire to father a male heir four centuries later.

Henry's request to Pope Clement VII to annul his first marriage, enabling him to take a new and hopefully male-child-bearing queen, was denied, and his solution was to order the Archbishop of Canterbury to grant him a divorce. This extreme measure led to Henry breaking with the Roman Catholic Church and establishing himself as Supreme Head of the Church of England. He promptly ordered the destruction of the country's powerful monasteries and religious houses, which enabled him to both stamp out their papist influence and, as an added bonus, procure their vast wealth and property.

"I desired to live worthily as long as I lived, and to leave after my life, to the men who should come after me, the memory of me in good works." —*Alfred the Great*

THE SEARCH FOR ALFRED'S BONES

Hyde Abbey's turn for demolition came in 1538, and soon there was nothing left to be seen above ground; however, Alfred's crypt was left undisturbed beneath the earth—until 1788, when a "bridewell" (a prison or house of correction for petty offenders) was constructed on the site. According to a contemporary eyewitness account, the royal graves were emptied and the bones scattered. Around eighty years later, the rector of St Bartholomew's Church in Hyde purchased a collection of bones, claimed by the vendor to be those of Alfred and his family, and reinterred them in an unmarked grave.

In 2013, the church and Hyde 900, a community cultural group, were granted permission to exhume the remains, but disappointingly they proved to date from at least 1100—by that time Alfred had been dead for two hundred years. More promising, however, was a fragment of pelvic bone, including the right hip joint, unearthed at the location of the high altar during an excavation of the Hyde Abbey site in the last years of the twentieth century and stored in a box in the city's Museum Service. Radiocarbon dating and osteological analysis revealed the bone to date back to between 895 and 1017 and to have belonged to a man aged between 26 and 45 or more at death. It is just feasible, then, that this precious bone belonged to King Alfred himself, and hope springs eternal that further community digs will persuade the earth to relinquish the great king's skeleton in its entirety.

Alfred's legacy. A page from the last will and testament of Alfred the Great, drawn up almost fifteen years before his death.

Which one is Alfred? The bones believed to be those of the king and his family, reinterred in a Winchester churchyard in the nineteenth century.

HAROLD II

1066 is the most famous year in English history, William the Conqueror among the most famous names, and Hastings among the most famous battles. That year, William of Normandy crossed the English Channel, his mission to claim the throne from Harold II. William was successful; Harold lost the battle and his life—but where are his remains?

**Harold II (Godwinson),
king of England**
Born: c.1020
Reigned: Jan–Oct 1066
Spouse: Edith (Ealdgyth) Swan-Neck
Died: 1066 at the Battle of Hastings
Successor: William the Conqueror

HAROLD GODWINSON, Earl of Wessex, was destined to become—albeit briefly—the last of the Anglo-Saxon kings, a line that included the outstanding ruler Alfred the Great. As the pious and childless Edward the Confessor (r.1042–66) lay on his deathbed, he named Harold, his brother-in-law, as his successor—but Edward had already promised the throne to his distant cousin William, Duke of Normandy, some fifteen years earlier.

NO TIME TO WASTE

Harold, who had no royal bloodline in support of his accession and feared rival claims from both William and Harald Hardrada, king of Norway, wasted no time in having himself crowned king. The coronation took place on January 6, the day after Edward's death, in Westminster Abbey, founded by Edward in 1052 and consecrated in 1065. Harold was the first king to be crowned in the abbey and since then the coronation of every English monarch, with the exception of two (see p. 138), has been held there. Many monarchs are also buried in the abbey—but not Harold.

Saxons and Vikings

Harold II's reign came at the end of a complex period in English history. The Romans withdrew from Britain in 410 and over the next two hundred years Angles, Saxons, and Jutes invaded from Germany, forcing the native Britons into Scotland and Wales, and set up a number of warring kingdoms. The majority of these were eventually united under Egbert of Wessex, the first king of England (r.802–839). Soon, however, the Anglo-Saxons were themselves subjected to years of disruption by invaders, this time by the Vikings, whose first recorded raid took place in 787. Alfred the Great (r.871–899) kept the Vikings at bay, but they overran the country under the ineffectual rule of Ethelred II "the Unready" (r.979–1016) and a Danish king, Canute (r.1016–35), became king of all England. Under Canute's rule, Saxons and Vikings coexisted peacefully. But then came William …

The last Anglo-Saxon king. *Harold is illustrated here as part of a set of late nineteenth-century advertising cards produced for the UK cigarette manufacturer Wills.*

The shell of Battle Abbey. *All that remains of William the Conqueror's monastic foundation constructed on the site of the Battle of Hastings.*

If Harold wasted no time, neither did William of Normandy, who was furious at being deprived of the throne to which he had long been expecting to accede. He assembled an armada to carry his army and set sail for the south coast of England. He landed at Pevensey Bay in Sussex, completely unopposed—Harold, an unexpectedly talented commander, was fully occupied at the time defeating an invasion by Harald Hardrada at another famous battle—Stamford Bridge near York, in the north of England.

WILLIAM'S NORMAN ORIGINS

So what right had a Frenchman to claim the English throne? The answer lies in the fact that William was a Norman. Early in the tenth century, Viking raiders captured Rouen in northern France and were granted territory by the Frankish king. A hundred years later, the Vikings ruled a vast area—Terra Normannorum, "land of the men from the north." It was here that Edward the Confessor lived from age 10 to 35. His father was Ethelred II, his mother Emma of Normandy, who married King Canute after Ethelred's death. As king, Edward often consulted his Norman advisors—and promised the throne to William, illegitimate son and heir of Duke Robert of Normandy, dubbed "the Magnificent."

The Bayeux Tapestry. *Embroidered in eight colors, the work measures more than 230 feet/ 70 meters long, nearly 20 inches/ 0.5 meter wide. Here, Harold receives his deathblow.*

THE BATTLE OF HASTINGS

The confrontation between William and Harold took place on October 14, 1066. Their armies each

Bayeux Tapestry

The *Bayeux Tapestry* is an intricate embroidered work depicting the Battle of Hastings. More than 230 feet/70 meters long and stitched in woolen yarns on linen, it is thought to have been commissioned by William's half-brother, Bishop Odo of Bayeux. One scene illustrates a Saxon warrior being struck in the eye by an arrow; above the image is the word "Harold," and according to legend this is how the king met his death.

comprised around seven thousand soldiers; Harold's men, all on foot, formed a defensive shield on a high ridge, while William's army, of both infantry and cavalry, was tasked with scaling the hill and breaching the human wall. The Normans' initial assault failed; however, William then engaged cunning tactics and achieved victory through a cleverly orchestrated two-pronged attack on the English army by archers and infantrymen, followed by a cavalry charge. By evening, the struggle was over, William the Bastard was now William the Conqueror, and Harold was lying dead on the battlefield.

EDITH SWAN-NECK

Enter a new character in this most dramatic and significant of historic events—Edith Swan-Neck, an Anglo-Danish noblewoman with swan-white skin, a symbol of beauty, whom Harold had "married" in a handfasting ceremony. Edith picked her way for hours through the mutilated corpses on the battlefield, searching for the body of her husband, which she eventually discovered; although Harold had been stripped of his regal insignia, Edith identified him by certain marks on his body. Harold's mother offered her son's weight in gold for the return of his remains, but William refused to surrender the body for burial.

> "She knew the secret marks on his body better than others did, for she had been admitted to a greater intimacy of his person." —*Waltham Chronicle, c.1180*

WHO HAS HAROLD?

William was apparently not completely heartless; in 1070 he began to build an abbey on the site of the battle, with its high altar on the spot where Harold fell. A stone slab now marks the place, amid the ruins of Battle Abbey. But where is Harold himself? One theory suggests that he did not die at Hastings at all, but lived on into old age as a hermit. Another idea is that he was buried at Waltham Abbey in Essex, south England, and yet another that only his head and heart were taken there while his torso was buried under Holy Trinity Church in Bosham in Sussex. Or perhaps the truth, as many suspect, is that his corpse was simply spirited away by William's troops and buried in a place where no one would ever find it, in order to prevent his grave becoming a shrine and pilgrim destination … All that is known for certain is that Harold's final resting place remains a mystery.

A gruesome search. *Edith Swan-Neck locates Harold's body. William had allowed the two clerics with her to search for Harold but they were unable to identify him among the dead.*

HENRY I

The English king Henry I's reign allegedly came to an undignified end when he devoured a surfeit of lampreys, a delicacy beloved of the medieval aristocracy. He was buried in Reading Abbey, where a project is currently afoot to restore the crumbling ruins—and perhaps unearth the bones of Henry, whose tomb is thought to have been destroyed in the sixteenth century.

Henry I ("Beauclerc")
Born: 1069, Selby, England
Reigned: 1100–35
Spouses: 1. Matilda of Scotland (m. 1100); 2. Adeliza of Louvain (m. 1121)
Children: Matilda (b. 1102), William (b. 1103)
Died: December 1, 1135, Lyons la Forêt, France
Buried: 1136, Reading, England
Successor: Stephen

HENRY "BEAUCLERC" WAS BORN in 1069, the fourth and youngest son of William I, the Conqueror. Henry's kingship came about through the untimely death of his brother William II, the Conqueror's nominated heir. Another brother, Richard, had predeceased his father, and Henry's eldest brother, Robert, was on crusade when William II died. Henry seized the moment, promptly snatched the royal treasure, and had himself crowned.

ENERGETIC, DECISIVE, AND OCCASIONALLY CRUEL

After seizing the English throne in 1066, Henry's grandfather, William I, implemented many significant changes to the country's social, political, and spiritual landscape. He also altered the physical landscape—designating royal forests for hunting and building castles, cathedrals, and the famous Tower of London. He confiscated land from the existing Anglo-Saxon nobility to give to his Norman followers and defeated any attempts at revolt. His successor, William II, followed in his footsteps to an extent, but ironically he was killed by an arrow while hunting in his father's "New Forest"—apparently accidentally, although the indecent haste with which Henry then claimed the throne casts doubt.

The Anarchy
Henry I's demise sparked a succession crisis. His son William had drowned in 1120, aged 17, when the ship in which he was returning from France, *La Blanche Nef*, was wrecked. Henry then named his daughter Matilda as his heir, but when he died his nephew Stephen usurped the throne, with the support of the English barons, who did not relish the idea of being ruled by a woman. Nineteen years of brutal civil war between Stephen and Matilda followed, known as the Anarchy, and although Matilda finally withdrew, it was her son who succeeded Stephen.

The Good Scholar. *Painted nearly five hundred years after his death, by an unknown artist, this portrait of Henry I, the "good scholar," hangs in the National Portrait Gallery in London.*

Described by historians as "energetic, decisive, and occasionally cruel," Henry was also a very effective ruler. He was well educated, as his byname "Beauclerc" ("good scholar") indicates, and he was the first Norman king to speak fluent English. He issued a Charter of Liberties, promising his subjects good governance, and instituted legal and administrative reforms. He also instigated a meritocracy, appointing talented low-born individuals to administrative roles at court. Through his marriage to Matilda of Scotland he established a lull in the turbulent relationship between the two countries. His relationship with his surviving brother, Robert, Duke of Normandy, was less peaceful, however, and in 1106 Henry imprisoned Robert and took control of Normandy. It was at Lyons la Forêt, not far from Normandy's capital, Rouen, that Henry is said to have indulged in his last meal of lampreys, a sinister-looking jawless fish, and succumbed to a fatal bout of food poisoning.

Henry mourns his son. A *poignant miniature of Henry mourning the loss of his only legitimate son and heir, William, in the sinking of* La Blanche Nef (The White Ship) *in 1120.*

HENRY'S MAUSOLEUM

On June 23, 1121, Henry laid the foundation stone of Reading Abbey. It was here that he wished to be buried—specifically, before the high altar in the choir, where the monks would pray for his soul. Accordingly, on Henry's death, his body needed to be shipped back to England; but because he died in early December, and a delay was expected before safe passage could be made, his entrails, heart, eyes, and brain were removed, since they were likely to rot, and buried in a priory near Rouen. The rest of his body was embalmed and wrapped in a bull's hide for transportation to Reading, where his funeral took place with great ceremony in January 1136. A splendid monument was erected and Henry was left to rest in peace, with a lamp perpetually burning—but only for four hundred years.

The martyrdom of Hugh Faringdon. *The unfortunate abbot of Reading at the time of Henry VIII's dissolution of the monasteries was indicted for high treason and put to death.*

AN ACT OF WILLFUL DESTRUCTION

At New Year 1532, another Henry—Henry VIII, a regular visitor to Reading Abbey—presented numerous gifts to the abbot. Yet by the end of the decade Reading Abbey had been ransacked and largely destroyed in Henry's dissolution of England's monasteries, and that same abbot convicted of high treason; his punishment was to be hanged, drawn, and quartered in front of his own church, his severed limbs flung into a cauldron of boiling pitch. The abbey buildings were robbed of their lead, glass, and facing stones, leaving only the vulnerable core, which gradually decayed into ruin.

And what of poor Henry I, disturbed in his rest in the abbey that he founded? The story, perhaps apocryphal, is that the iconoclasts who rampaged around the country demolishing monastic buildings believed Henry to be entombed in a silver casket, and that in their disappointment at discovering nothing more valuable than a stone sarcophagus, they simply scattered his bones to the four winds.

"The corpse ... well rubbed and saturated with salt, was inclosed in a bull's hide." —Decem Scriptores, 1339

THE HIDDEN ABBEY PROJECT

Another four hundred years have passed, and the truth—or untruth—of this tale could soon be revealed. Archaeologists and historians plan to use ground-penetrating radar to detect the full extent of the once powerful and magnificent abbey complex. This will be followed, where possible, by keyhole and trial trench investigation. There is hope that an archaeological dig will reveal Henry's tomb to be intact and his remains still where they were laid all those centuries ago, exactly as he wished. If not, his fate may remain forever unknown.

The ruins of Reading Abbey. *Archaeologists using ground-penetrating radar have located graves near the location of the High Altar, but to date Henry I's remains have not been found.*

GENGHIS KHAN

Genghis Khan, the great Mongol conqueror, is often dubbed the cruelest man in history and was responsible for tens of millions of deaths. Today he is revered by Mongolians as a cultural hero—establisher not only of a vast empire but also of Mongolian identity. They often refer to themselves as "Genghis Khan's children." Yet there is no known record of exactly how Genghis himself died—or where he was buried. The impressive three-domed Genghis Khan Mausoleum in north China is nothing more than a red herring, containing his possessions but not his remains …

Temüjin/Genghis Khan
Born: *c.* 1162, near Lake Baikal, Mongolia
Spouse: Börte (m. *c.* 1227); plus other morganatic wives
Children: Jochi, Chagatai, Ogedei, Tolui (plus countless children with other morganatic wives, including at least six daughters
Died: August 18, 1227, northern China
Mausoleum: Ordos, Inner Mongolia

THE BOY TEMÜJIN who was to become Genghis Khan was born into a nomadic life in the harsh and hostile environment of the Mongolian steppe, where the temperature ranges are extreme and the winds unforgiving. Despite this unpromising start, his was, according to tradition, a divine destiny; legend also has it that he was born holding in his hand a clot of blood, an auspicious sign—or perhaps merely a portent of what was to befall his unfortunate victims.

TEMÜJIN BECOMES CHINGGIS

Temüjin's potential for cruelty manifested early on—apparently, as a young teenager, he killed his half-brother in an argument, ostensibly over nothing more than possession of a fish, although the possibility that his sibling stood between Temüjin and succession to their late father's role as head of a clan seems a more likely motivation. The adolescent Temüjin also displayed other signs of not being a man to mess with—for example, he pursued thieves who had stolen his family's horses and retrieved them, and when his wife (a comparatively "older woman" whom he married at the age of 16) was abducted by a rival clan, he assembled a large army to retrieve her, too.

But Temüjin also showed early signs of effective leadership, inspiring others to help him even in the most unlikely of circumstances, such as when he was captured by a rival tribe and one of his captors aided his escape at considerable risk to his own life. The noble council of the Mongolian clans was impressed by Temüjin's brave deeds and in 1206 proclaimed him their overall leader, awarding

Face of a conqueror. *This portrait of Genghis Khan in the National Palace Museum in Taipei, Taiwan, is recognized as the most accurate image of the Mongol leader.*

A family affair. Genghis Khan enthroned with his sons, Ogedei and Jochi, depicted in a Persian manuscript.

him the title Genghis (Chinggis) Khan. Both names had a deterministic flavor—Temüjin translates as "of iron" and Genghis Khan as "supreme ruler" or "universal ruler." This tall, strong man—who, according to accounts, had an impressive mane of hair and a long bushy beard—certainly went on to rule with a rod of iron.

GHENGIS'S ARMY

Genghis was extremely clever about assembling his vast army. One hundred thousand strong, it was divided on decimal principles into ten-man platoons in a one hundred-man company, with one thousand in a brigade and ten thousand in a division. Officers were appointed his officers on the basis of their skill and experience, or even just their honesty—a soldier who had owned up to shooting Genghis's horse in a tribal battle and nearly killing Genghis himself was rewarded with a high rank. With this army of completely loyal and devoted supporters behind him, Genghis set about leading them in a series of conquests that would result in history's largest empire on contiguous land.

THE CONQUEST UNFOLDS

Genghis began his campaign by subjugating the Tangut tribe of Xixia in northwestern China, and after that there was no stopping him. He exhibited tactical brilliance in dealing with resistance—his solution when coming up against the impressive defenses of Peking (Beijing) in 1215 was to starve the citizens into submission. Not only did he make extensive use of then-popular weapons such as siege engines and burning oil in his quest to take cities, he was even prepared to divert rivers to deprive the inhabitants of water.

"I am the punishment of God. ... If you had not committed great sins, God would not have sent a punishment like me upon you." —*Genghis Khan*

Genghis was an intelligent man, who learned a great deal from those he conquered; and as long as a conquered kingdom succumbed to Mongol rule, he was also a happy man. Resist him, however, and it was a very different story. In 1219, the Khwarezm-Shah broke a trade agreement to exchange goods along the historic Silk Road, which had linked China with Rome since the first century BCE, and massacred a caravan of Muslim merchants under Genghis's protection. It was a foolish move. The Khwarezmid territories in Persia (modern-day Iran) found themselves under attack by the Mongol hordes. Millions were killed, the Shah's empire was no more, and to emphasize his point, Genghis then annihilated the Tangut tribe, his first conquest, who had (equally foolishly) refused to supply troops for the invasion. For good measure, he ordered the execution of the whole Tangut royal family to punish them for their defiance. Hell hath no fury like a conqueror scorned.

OFF WITH THEIR HEADS!

The prospect alone of a Mongol invasion was an effective weapon, and Genghis was reputedly fond of displaying his decapitated victims as a warning to those who might think of defying him. It has been estimated that during his twenty-year reign of terror he murdered nearly forty million; there is even an apocryphal tale of him killing 1,748,000 people in Nishapur, Persia, within the space of one hour (an average of 29,133 people per minute) in revenge for the death of his favorite son-in-law. While the speed of the slaughter is exaggerated, and it is unlikely that Genghis himself was the executioner, it is known to have taken place—no living being was spared, including women, children, babies, cats, and dogs, and the severed skulls were piled into gruesome pyramids. However, as fast as Genghis was reducing the population, he was planting his seed to guarantee its regeneration—a 2003 study concluded that around sixteen million people alive today can claim to be his descendants.

Genghis rides again. *This huge 131-foot/40-meter steel statue of Genghis Khan on horseback was completed in 2008. It is located on the bank of the Tuul River east of the Mongolian capital Ulaanbaatar and dominates the steppes of Mongolia.*

THE MYSTERY OF GENGHIS'S DEATH

Genghis Khan died in northern China on August 18, 1227, and like other remarkable conquerors before him, his life is thought to have come to a somewhat unremarkable end. The date is certain, but how he died is less so. Traditionally, the cause was injuries sustained after falling from his horse, although an illness or a minor wound from an arrow are also possible, or even that he was murdered for trying to impose his unwanted attentions on a Chinese princess. Whatever the cause of death, his enemies, relieved to hear of his demise, described him as "Accursed of God."

THE MOBILE MAUSOLEUM

Even more mysterious than the cause of his death, however, is what happened to Genghis afterward. A mausoleum houses his personal effects—his saddle, his bow, and similar items—as a focus for worship in the Mongol tradition. His grandson, Kublai Khan, charged the Darhad Mongol tribe with guarding the mausoleum, and it has been in their care since 1696. Originally, the relics were housed inside eight white yurts, which could be moved in times of warfare, for example; but in the 1950s a permanent site was constructed, containing copies of the relics, most of which had long since been lost or stolen. Fiercely proud of their most famous ruler, the Mongolians now hold four memorial ceremonies a year at the mausoleum—sacrificial gifts are offered and there are traditional activities such as archery, horse racing, and wrestling.

The Great Khan in battle. Mongolian horses were relatively small but extremely hardy, with a great deal of stamina.

Mausoleum but no body. The permanent mausoleum building in Ordos Prefecture, Inner Mongolia, designed to resemble three Mongolian yurts (central section only shown).

ETERNAL BLUE HEAVEN

But where are the actual remains, the bones of Genghis Khan? The little information we have is based on folklore and legend. For centuries, the location has been unknown—and it seems Genghis went to great lengths to ensure that it would never be known. Very great lengths, in fact: It is said that those in his funeral procession were instructed to slaughter any potential witnesses they encountered on the journey, and having buried their leader they were to trample the earth covering the grave beneath their horses' hooves to conceal it. According to another tradition, his tomb was concealed by diverting a river over it, and some believe its location is protected by a curse.

Despite this, many efforts have been made to find the remains of Genghis Khan, some involving ground-penetrating radar, global positioning devices, and satellite imaging. In 2016, Robin Ackroyd, a British freelance journalist, published a book in which he claimed to have found the long-lost tomb, high on a mountain—not in the Ordos region of China where Genghis died, but in northern Mongolia. The location, the Burkhan Khaldun mountain, has been a UNESCO World Heritage site since 2015. Ackroyd believes Genghis was repatriated after his death and that his lofty choice of location was a reflection of Mongol spiritual belief—and if he is right, then the twist in the tale of Genghis Khan is that this notorious butcher was actually a highly spiritual being, laid to rest in the realm of the Mongols' supreme deity whom he worshipped, the Eternal Blue Heaven.

A spiritual slaughterer?

Surprisingly for one so violent, Genghis Khan embraced rather than suppressed the spiritual traditions of those he conquered. In the Mongol region a traditional shamanistic belief system was observed. Genghis was both tolerant of and curious about all the faiths he encountered—including Buddhism, Nestorian Christianity, and Islam. He even enjoyed conversing with the Taoist sage Qiu Chuji, although what the latter would have made of Genghis's plans to conquer China will never be known.

VLAD TEPES, "THE IMPALER"

Vlad III was a fifteenth-century prince of Wallachia, a land that is now part of Romania, north of the Danube and south of the wild Carpathian mountains. He lived at a time when the peoples of the lands that are now Eastern Europe were in a continual state of conflict with the Ottoman Empire. So how did his name come to be adopted as that of a fictional vampire count, anti-hero of one of the best-loved Gothic novels ever written?

Vladislas III, prince of Wallachia, known as Dracula, son of Dracul
Born: 1431, probably in Sighisoara, Transylvania
Spouses: (1) name unknown, died 1462; (2) Ilona Szilagyi, dates unknown
Died: Disappeared in battle, probably killed, 1476

THE REAL VLAD was the son of Vlad II, a *voivode*, or minor ruler, in Wallachia. In the year of Vlad III's birth, his father became a knight in the Order of the Dragon under the sponsorship of Sigismond, king of Hungary. As a result, Vlad II added "Dracul" (the Hungarian word for dragon) to his name, and his son duly became "Dracula," son of dracul.

WAR WITH THE OTTOMANS

To be a knight in the Order of the Dragon was no mere formality: The order had a cause and a purpose, which was to defeat the Ottoman Empire. Wallachia was the buffer state between the Christian European countries and the Muslim Ottomans, and thus frequently became a battleground when the two sides clashed.

Not much is known of Vlad's early childhood, but we know that at the age of 11 he accompanied his father to a meeting with the Ottoman sultan Murad II, and was promptly taken hostage with his brother Radu, to be held as a guarantee of their father's good behavior.

HELD BY THE TURKS

Although Vlad and Radu couldn't leave court, they were treated as guests rather than prisoners, and were extensively educated in the arts and sciences, and in skills such as horsemanship. While Radu converted to Islam, Vlad consistently refused, remaining committed to his original Christian faith.

Grim countenance. *Painted during the second half of the sixteenth century, this famous—and rather grim—portrait of Vlad Tepes is believed to be a copy of an earlier picture, possibly a portrait taken from life.*

The Impaler's victims.

A contemporary German woodcut showing the Impaler in action. Vlad enjoys his meal, looking on as his henchmen deal with his enemies.

The brothers weren't set free until after the death of their father, more than five years after they had first been taken captive. Back in Wallachia, Vlad II had been battling a rebellion by the noble families of the region. He was eventually caught and killed in 1447, and his position was usurped by one of the Wallachian nobles. When he was finally released from the Ottoman court, Vlad III fought to win back his father's lands and status, but although he succeeded, his triumph was brief—after only two months, he was unseated once again.

BECOMING "THE IMPALER"

After losing his Wallachian power base, Vlad drops out of history, unrecorded, for a few years. In the meantime, Sigismond of Hungary died and was replaced by Ladislaus V, and in 1453 something happened that the Christian forces of Europe had long dreaded: Constantinople, eastern center of the Christian faith, fell to the Turks. Threatened with a full-scale invasion westward, the forces of the border countries, including Wallachia, rose against the enemy, and Vlad reappears in 1456, once again *voivode* in his home country, although still dogged by uprisings and opposition, and constantly plagued by a range of pretenders. The first we hear of him is that he refuses to pay tribute to the Turkish sultan—a longstanding "tax" against invasion. This in itself was an act of provocation to the Ottoman ruler. Soon after, he decided to take vengeance on the noblemen who had risen against his father. He invited them to a great feast, promoting it as a gesture of reconciliation; when the guests arrived, Vlad's men fell upon them, murdered them, and impaled their bodies on lances. A lurid but popular range of German woodcuts, produced not long after the event, show an untroubled Vlad enjoying his meal surrounded by these unfortunates, the stakes sunk into the ground around his table.

Impaling, and other horrors

Inflicting horrible and creative deaths on one's enemies was far from unusual in the fifteenth century. Crucifixion, drawing and quartering, and chopping off limbs were all accepted punishments designed not only to torment the victims but to raise fear in any who might think of following them in opposing a ruler or regime. A gifted torturer could make a victim last longer by driving the stake lengthwise up through the body, placing it between the ribs so as to avoid damaging the liver or the heart—thus ensuring that, although in terrible pain, the victims wouldn't die immediately. If time was short, the stake was simply driven through the center of the body, making for a quicker death. The punishments meted out by Vlad were deemed harsh but fair rather than barbaric: Contemporaries celebrated him as a hero and a patriot.

THE LAST CONFLICTS

Having conquered his local enemies, Vlad looked to extend his power base further afield. At a meeting with envoys from the Turkish sultan, sent to broker peace, he asked them to remove their turbans. When they declared their religion would not allow it, he congratulated them on their piety—and instructed his men to seize the envoys and to nail their turbans to their heads, thus ensuring they could never take them off. And he continued to impale his enemies, whether they were local noblemen or Ottoman soldiers captured in the course of their regular incursions onto Vlad's territory. In 1462, the Ottoman army led by Mehmet II managed to reach Wallachia's capital city, Targoviste. On arrival they found it eerily deserted but completely surrounded by a forest of stakes—upon closer inspection it could be seen that each and every one bore the body of an Ottoman prisoner of war.

"Oh, what grace they exhibit!" —Attributed to Vlad III, *as he watched his victims writhing on their stakes*

Vlad never regained his status and power fully, and spent regular periods in exile from Wallachia, nonetheless constantly engaging in battle with the encroaching Turkish forces. He is believed to have died in an ambush in 1476, after which his body disappeared.

WHERE'S THE BODY?

Although the Impaler was something of a local hero in Wallachia, Vlad's grave has never been reliably located. For a long time it was believed that he had been buried in the church at Snagov Monastery—near the outskirts of modern Bucharest. Situated on a small island, accessible only by boat, Snagov could certainly claim strong links with Vlad when he was alive—he is believed to have used it as a center of operations at times, and was responsible not only for the fortifications that at one time enclosed the monastery, but also for a bell tower and for the erection of a new church built there during his lifetime. More characteristically, he also installed a jail and a torture chamber on the island. Despite these links, a rival claim to be the site of Vlad's burial has also been

Possible tomb? *The church at Piazza Santa Maria, Naples, contains the supposed tomb of Vlad Tepes, shown on the left. The rampant dragon in the middle of the facade encouraged the belief of Estonian scholars that it might be Dracula's final resting place.*

Snagov Monastery. Traditionally believed to be Vlad's final resting place and located some 20 miles/32 kilometers from Bucharest, the fourteenth-century monastery stands on a small island at the northern end of Lake Snagov and can only be reached by boat. Despite the controversy over the authenticity of the burial place, the interior of the church contains both a plaque and a portrait of the original Dracula.

made for Comana Monastery, on the grounds that it stands nearer to the site of the ambush in which he is supposed to have perished. Both versions of the story held that he had been buried headless—his head having been carried off as a trophy and taken to Constantinople as proof to the sultan that his enemy was dead. When it reached its destination, legend has it that the sultan caused Vlad's head to be impaled on a stake and paraded around the city. In 2014, however, a team of scholars from the University of Tallinn, in Estonia, threw an unexpected curveball into the mix. They declared that Vlad's true tomb had been located a very long way from home—in a church in Piazza Santa Maria in Naples. The theory went that a tomb, which had always been assumed to be that of an anonymous Italian nobleman, was covered with significant carvings, and that the symbolism of these pointed to an illustrious inhabitant hailing from the Carpathians—a dragon standing for Dracula,

"The last I saw of Count Dracula was his kissing his hand to me, with a red light of triumph in his eyes, and with a smile that Judas in hell might be proud of." —Dracula, *Bram Stoker*

and two sphinxes symbolizing Thebes—wordplay for "Tepes." Sadly, the academics' argument failed to convince the authorities that the tomb should be opened, and Vlad's final resting place remains a cause for debate.

AFTERLIFE: THE INSPIRATION FOR DRACULA THE VAMPIRE

There is a substantial footnote to the life and death of the Wallachian bogeyman. Away from his native land, today Vlad is best known as the inspiration for Bram Stoker's *Dracula*, published in 1897. Stoker is said to have found his inspiration for the undead count in a book with the decidedly unsensational title *Account of the Principalities of Wallachia and Moldavia*. It wasn't an exciting tome, although it apparently contained many accounts of local legends, but somewhere in its footnotes was a mention that "Dracula in the Wallachian language means Devil." After he had read the account, Stoker later complained to his son, Irving, that he had had an exceptionally vivid and unpleasant dream—although he blamed it, not on dark forces, but on the fact that he had eaten "too much dressed crab."

Vampires were by no means unique to Stoker: They were already common currency in sensational novels by the end of the nineteenth century, and one of the first, *Varney the Vampire, or the Feast of Blood*, had been serialized as early as 1845. Stoker, though, was looking for more—not just an eerie personality for his protagonist, but also a suitably remote location in which to place him. A castle in the Carpathians, wreathed in mist and surrounded by the mournful howls of wolves, made a perfect background for the sinister count. Once Stoker's decision was made, adding a fog of menace was simple enough—and the fictional Dracula was born. Unlike Vlad who, wherever he is, is certainly well and truly dead, Stoker's Count lives on wherever he can find a taste for literary horror.

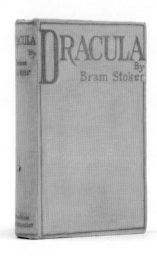

A legend is born. *The first edition of Bram Stoker's* Dracula.

The memorial to Vlad. *A tribute to Vlad Tepes stands among architectural fragments at the Museum of the Old Princely Court in Bucharest. The Court, now ruined, was built in the mid-fifteenth century on Vlad's orders.*

VLAD TEPES
1456–1562

THOMAS PAINE

In his lifetime he was famous—or notorious—for his radical opinions and revolutionary writings: equally feted and reviled in England, France, and America. So how was it that Thomas Paine died lonely and almost unknown, and how did his bones end up scattered all over the world?

Thomas Paine
Born: February 9, 1737, Thetford, Norfolk, England
Spouses: Mary Lambert (m. September 27, 1759); Elizabeth Ollive (m. March 26, 1771)
Children: None surviving
Died: June 8, 1809, Greenwich Village, New York

THERE WAS NOTHING in Thomas Paine's background that indicated he would be exceptional. Born Thomas Pain (he added an "e" in adulthood) in Thetford, a market town in the east of England, his parents lived modestly; his father, a Quaker, smallholder, and "staymaker"—the technical term for a maker of ropes, although later in life it would lead Paine's detractors to mock him as a maker of stays for ladies' corsets—was determined that his only son would have an education. Paine junior attended the local school until he was 13, when he was taken into his father's business. However, he worked with his father for just three years before, at the age of 16, going to sea on a privateer, or ship-for-hire, on which he served for—accounts vary—between three and six years.

EARLY FAILURES

In 1759, at the age of 22, Paine returned to England. Thereafter his early life can be summed up succinctly: For the next two decades he experimented with various livings but nothing that he tried seemed to meet with any success. First he set up his own rope-making business in Sandwich, a coastal town in southern England, where he married his first wife, Mary Lambert, who died with her baby in childbirth just a year later. After her death Paine moved back to his parents' home to study for a new career as an excise officer, collecting duties on imported goods. He moved north for his first job in the new role, but was fired in 1765, after claims that he had signed for goods that he had not actually inspected. An unsettled period followed when he returned to rope-making, then worked first as a servant and then as a teacher in London. In 1768, he worked as an excise officer once more, moving to the small town of Lewes, where he lived above a tobacconist's shop. And it was here that his political interests were first seriously roused.

POLITICAL AWAKENING

During his six years in Lewes, Paine became a member of both the Society of Twelve, a local group who managed services for the town, and the Headstrong Club, a local drinking club whose members met weekly to discuss the great issues of the day. It was the first hint that Paine might take a practical interest in politics,

Thomas Paine. *This portrait was painted by American artist John Wesley Jarvis (nephew of Methodist founder John Wesley) in c.1805. Jarvis was interested in studying Paine's skull after his death—but his subject firmly rejected the idea.*

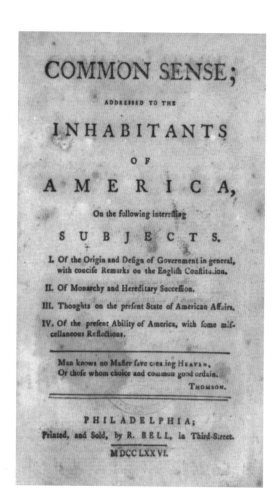

Common Sense. *The first edition, addressed to the "inhabitants of America," was published anonymously in Philadelphia in 1776.*

and in 1772 he authored his first paper, "The Case of the Officers of Excise," an appeal to Parliament for better pay and conditions for excise officers. Radical for its time, it went down badly with his employers and when Paine was accused of being absent from his post without permission, he was fired—for the second and final time. Penniless and in danger of being sent to debtors' prison, he sold all his possessions to settle what he owed, formally separated from his second wife, Elizabeth, and moved to London.

A LIFE'S VOCATION

By 1774, at the age of 37, Paine had come of age politically but had lost his family and his living. However, he had found his direction in life: In London he became an occasional pamphleteer on current events. Pamphleteers wielded a good deal of influence in eighteenth-century London. They offered the most direct form of social and political comment available, and Paine quickly revealed himself to be a political radical who was adept at putting his points across. Serendipitously a friend introduced him to Benjamin Franklin, who was living in London at the time and suggested Paine travel to America, where his skills would be in demand. Paine set sail in October 1774. Typhus broke out on the ship and he narrowly avoided death on the voyage; on arrival at Philadelphia, he had to be carried onto the quay. Franklin had alerted his contacts with warmly worded letters of recommendation, and as soon as Paine had recovered his strength he found employment, first writing for *Pennsylvania Magazine*, a vehicle for political reform, and a little later being appointed its editor. His writings became known to the great reforming names of the day: Thomas Jefferson and John and Samuel Adams all read and praised them.

Early in 1776, *Common Sense*, one of his most famous works, was published. It presented a powerful argument for the American colonies to be given independence from British rule, and its author became celebrated in revolutionary circles. By the summer, he was working as a war correspondent as the War of Independence took shape, and his "Crisis Papers" were read to inspire the troops during the bitter winter of 1776. From this point on, he played a key role in the conflict, traveling to France to negotiate a war loan in 1781 and joining in Washington's victory march down Broadway at the end of the Revolutionary War in November 1783. Recognizing the value of his role, the new Congress rewarded him with a farm in New Rochelle, New York State, and a payment of $3,000.

"Poor Tom Paine! There he lies:
Nobody laughs and nobody cries
Where he has gone or how he fares
Nobody knows and nobody cares."

—*Popular rhyme in circulation after Paine's death*

A DECADE IN FRANCE

The 1780s saw Paine's interests take a new direction: Although he kept writing, he also designed a single-span iron bridge, groundbreaking for the period. He also paid a visit to his mother back in Thetford, and spent time on his farm in New York.

However, in 1789 the outbreak of the French Revolution caused ripples all over Europe and when the philosopher and writer Edmund Burke published his attack on the revolutionaries—*Reflections on the Revolution in France*—it was inevitable that Paine would feel compelled to write a response. In March 1791, he published his most radical work yet, the first part of *Rights of Man*, an argument for republican government that promptly sold almost a million copies in England. This aggravated the British government to the point of issuing a writ against its author for "wicked and seditious writings" and convicting him in his absence—Paine was by now in France, where he lived for much of the following decade, seeing the results of the Revolution at first hand.

Paine became embroiled in conflict between factions, incurring the deadly wrath of Maximilien Robespierre, one of the leading revolutionaries. At one point he escaped execution by a hair's breadth—during his incarceration in the Luxembourg prison in Paris, a jailer, chalking the rooms of those who were to be executed the following day, accidentally marked the inside rather than the outside of Paine's door. Paine survived the fall of Robespierre and reversed his fortunes sufficiently to become a member of the French Convention (the assembly that governed France) in 1795, and remained in the country until 1802, long enough to watch the rise of Napoleon (who fulsomely declared himself an admirer—"a statue of gold should be erected to you in every city in the universe") and to deplore the latter's evident aspirations to a dictatorship. Toward the end of the 1790s, he was living with the family of Nicolas de Bonneville, a printer and journalist who was his close friend.

Common Nonsense. *In this satirical cartoon opposing Paine, published in London in 1792, his "halo" is made up of treason, perdition, and murder, while his scroll reads "Common Nonsense."*

RETURN TO AMERICA

The turn of the century had changed much in America. Paine, never slow to fall out with previous allies, had felt betrayed by George Washington who, when president, had done nothing to save him during his imprisonment in France. Paine's return to the US in 1802, accompanied by Bonneville's wife Marguerite Brazier and her sons, was at the invitation of Thomas Jefferson, who had become president the previous year. (Bonneville, who had fallen out of favor with Napoleon, nevertheless remained in France, living precariously.) Paine was no longer popular, disliked for his godlessness by the religious and for his republicanism by the Federalists—perhaps, like all revolutionaries in time, he had simply become unfashionable.

Paine's last years were lived in failing health, cared for devotedly by Marguerite Brazier, and on June 8, 1809, he died in Greenwich Village at the age of 72. His body was taken to La Rochelle in order to be buried in the graveyard of the Quaker community there, as requested in his will, but they rejected him. Eventually, he was interred under a walnut tree on his own property, the farm that had been given to him years earlier, with Marguerite Brazier taking care of the funeral arrangements.

FOR WANT OF A MEMORIAL

Paine was to rest in peace for only ten years. Enter William Cobbett. Cobbett, an English writer and agriculturalist with powerful political opinions and an occasional American resident, had for much of Paine's career been in vituperative opposition to him. After Paine's death, though, it weighed on Cobbett that such a prominent figure in history should lie in so obscure a spot. He decided that he would bring Paine's body back to his native land and would organize a subscription for a monument in St Paul's Cathedral, London—one that would be a more fitting memorial for someone who had played such an important part in so many people's fortunes.

The road to hell is paved with good intentions: Cobbett retrieved his fellow writer's remains in a blaze of publicity, and managed to get them on board a ship named either *Hercules* or *Elizabeth* (accounts vary) bound for Liverpool. Cobbett brought them back to England, where he gave a macabre dinner in their honor. He is also said to have made "memorial" rings containing hair clipped from Paine's rotting head, to offer to subscribers to the memorial venture—they were not a notable success.

Memorial plaque. On the wall of the White Hart Inn in Lewes, it commemorates Paine's life and celebrates his revolutionary fervor. He attended many of his earliest political meetings there.

THOMAS PAINE 1737–1809
HERE EXPOUNDED HIS REVOLUTIONARY POLITICS. THIS INN IS REGARDED AS A CRADLE OF AMERICAN INDEPENDENCE WHICH HE HELPED TO FOUND WITH PEN AND SWORD.

However, Cobbett had many troubles of his own. Already badly in debt, he was arrested and thrown into Newgate Prison just a few months after his arrival back in England. One of his collaborators in the Paine memorial scheme is said to have put the bones on public show for a few weeks— although few proved keen to visit them—after which they were placed in a box and stored in Cobbett's home. And when Cobbett died in 1835, the memorial subscription long forgotten, the bones were still there.

UP FOR AUCTION

Cobbett's effects were put up for auction at his farmhouse in Surrey, south of London, early in 1836. The skeleton was among them; when the box was opened, the auctioneer, horrified, refused to enter it in the sale. After the auction events become a little uncertain, but it is believed that the box of bones was given into the care of Cobbett's neighbor, George West, and that he gave them to Cobbett's old friend Benjamin Tilly, who kept them until he died himself in 1869.

At some point after this, the bones were separated. No one knows what became of them then: A contemporary story alleged that the larger bones had been sold to a button-maker and that "pieces of Paine" were fastening waistcoats and breeches all over London. This is unlikely, but what does seem certain is that by some means or other the bones were split up. Some claimed that they were sold, piecemeal, as mementos. In 1872, there was a sighting of Paine's alleged skull and right hand, which had made their way to Brighton, and into the study of the Reverend Ainslie, a Unitarian minister. In the 1980s Paine's skull was said to have arrived in Australia, but without DNA tests this could not be proved. Another rumor alleges that Paine, or at least most of him, came into the care of another Unitarian minister, the Reverend Alexander Gordon, and was given a discreet reburial in Manchester in the 1870s. The brain was (possibly) returned to La Rochelle, where it was kept in a secret location along with a lock of hair—soft, dark, and with a russet tinge, Paine had not gone gray—that had been taken from Paine shortly after his death. Back in London, with his bones scattered no one knew where, no memorial to Paine was ever built.

"In a way, it's poetic ... that his body is scattered ... This is the man who said 'The world is my country.'"—*Gary Berton, Thomas Paine National Historical Association, 2001*

Death mask. *Cast from his body in 1783, Thomas Paine's death mask was made by his friend, the artist John Wesley Jarvis, who had also painted his portrait in life.*

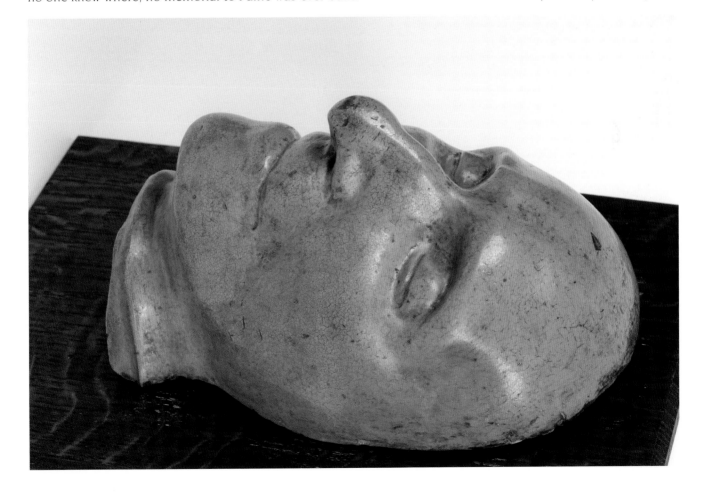

DAVY CROCKETT

Davy Crockett, dubbed the King of the Wild Frontier, was many things—frontiersman, politician, folk hero—but he is most famous for his death as a valiant volunteer soldier at the Battle of the Alamo, Texas. A tomb bearing Crockett's name stands in San Fernando Cathedral in San Antonio— but are the charred remains inside really his?

David Crockett
Born: August 17, 1786, Greene County, East Tennessee
Spouses: Mary Finley (m. 1806); Elizabeth Patton (m. 1815)
Children: John (b. 1807), William (b. 1808), Margaret (b. 1812), Robert (b. 1816), Rebecca (b. 1818), Matilda (b. 1821)
Died: March 6, 1836, San Antonio, Texas

DAVID CROCKETT WAS ILLITERATE until the age of 18, yet such was his charisma and witty oratorical skill that he went on to become a Congressman for the state of Tennessee, and it was even suggested that he should run for president. His popular image, however, is of "Davy," a rough, backwoods character in a fringed suede jacket and coonskin cap.

CROCKETT'S AMERICA

Crockett was born at the most exciting time in the settlement of North America. British colonization had been limited to the region along the eastern seaboard, but under the 1763 Treaty of Paris France ceded territory further inland—the fertile Ohio Valley, bordered to the west by the Mississippi River.

Expansion beyond the Appalachian Mountains continued to be restricted under the British crown's Proclamation of 1763, which was intended to protect Native American land rights, but when the 1783 Treaty of Paris recognized American independence from British rule, the floodgates were opened and settlers poured into Ohio, Tennessee, and Kentucky. The pioneers included John Crockett and his wife Rebecca, and in 1786 their fifth child, David, was born in their tiny cabin on the Nolichucky River in East Tennessee.

CROCKETT THE POLITICIAN

Raised in poverty, young Crockett was poorly educated, his childhood spent supplementing the family income as a farmhand; recognizing his disadvantage, he eventually taught himself to read and write. He married in 1806 and progressed further west into Tennessee with his wife and young family.

Conflict with the Native Americans was a constant feature of westward expansion—Crockett's own grandparents had been murdered by Creek and Cherokee tribal members before he was born, and he participated in the 1813–14 Creek War under the future United States president, Andrew Jackson. In the years that followed, he furthered his military career and also launched a political career.

A political force. A *formal portrait of David Crockett, whose career as a politician is often overlooked in favor of his more popular image as a backwoodsman.*

"King of the Wild Frontier."
It was in this guise that "Davy" Crockett was portrayed in Walt Disney's 1950s TV miniseries, with its catchy theme tune.

Crockett was twice elected to the Tennessee legislature, in 1821 and 1823, serving as a spokesman for impoverished settlers. Between 1825 and 1835 he ran five times for the US House of Representatives, first as a Democratic Jacksonian and then as a Whig, winning three times. In 1834, he published his autobiography, *A Narrative of the Life of David Crockett of the State of Tennessee*. A difference of opinion with Jackson over key issues, specifically the Indian Removal Act, led to his political downfall and he lost the 1835 election. His response was unequivocal: "You may all go to hell and I will go to Texas." It was here, in what he described as "the garden spot of the world," that he saw his future—but it was not to be.

THE ALAMO

Around 1718, Spanish settlers built the Mission San Antonio de Valera on the banks of the San Antonio River in Texas to house Christian missionaries. It was secularized in 1793, and ten years later Spanish soldiers from Mexico—the Second Flying Company of Álamo de Parras—were stationed in the abandoned chapel, their brief to protect the frontier against invasion by the United States. At that time there were only seventeen states officially in the Union, but the Louisiana Purchase of land from the French in 1803 effectively doubled the size of the young republic of America—and some of the land adjoined Spanish-controlled Texas, making it an obvious next target.

Over the coming years, the soldiers rebuilt and reinforced the mission compound, which became known as "the Alamo," and military troops occupied the fort on and off until the 1830s. During that time, Mexico gained its independence from Spain—but before that, the Spanish government had granted citizens of the US permission to settle in Texas, a province of Mexico. In October 1835, the Texians, as these settlers were known, launched their own bid for independence from Mexico, and two months later a group of Texian rebels overwhelmed the Mexican garrison at the Alamo and gained control of San Antonio and its fort.

THE SIEGE OF THE ALAMO

On February 23, a thousand or more soldiers, under the command of Mexico's military dictator General Antonio López de Santa Anna, arrived in San Antonio to put down the rebellion. The rebels withdrew to the Alamo, which was promptly surrounded by the Mexicans. Santa Anna raised a red flag as a signal that no mercy would be shown to those inside the mission. The besieged rebels, under the command of Lieutenant Colonel William B. Travis and Colonel James Bowie, numbered around one hundred and fifty and ranged in age from 16 to 56. They consisted of Texians, native Texans (known as Tejano), and volunteer soldiers including our hero, Davy Crockett, who had arrived in early February.

The Battle of the Alamo.
Only a few of the defenders survived the slaughter, and they were immediately executed on the orders of Santa Anna.

On February 24, Travis wrote a letter addressed to the People of Texas and All Americans in the World, begging them "in the name of Liberty, of patriotism & everything dear to the American character, to come to our aid, with all dispatch." He declared his intention to defend the fort to the last—"I shall never surrender or retreat"—and signed off with the stirring words "Victory or Death." Colonel Juan Seguín succeeded in carrying the letter through the enemy lines, but Travis's plea swelled the rebels' numbers by only thirty-two. There would have been more had not time, distance, and terrain hindered their arrival.

THE BATTLE OF THE ALAMO

Texas declared its independence on March 2, and four days later, just before dawn, the siege of the Alamo came to a violent end. The defenders were no match for the Mexican soldiers, who breached the walls and swarmed into the compound. Ninety minutes later, it was all over, not so much a battle as a massacre. Most who were not killed in the assault were dispatched soon afterward—but which of these tragic fates befell Crockett is both uncertain and contentious. The confusion stems from accounts that a handful of defenders had either surrendered or were captured, and were executed on Santa Anna's orders. There has been speculation that Crockett was among that number, diminishing his status as a courageous folk hero who went down fighting. A far more popular version of events finds him lying dead amid the

"This sacred spot, and those crumbling remains, the desecrated temple of Texian liberty will teach a lesson which freeman can never forget." —*Edward Burleson, Vice President of the Republic of Texas*

Remember the Alamo!
Santa Anna was himself defeated by Texian forces on April 21, in a battle that lasted just eighteen minutes and rang to the cry of "Remember the Alamo!" The words now appear on the reverse of the Texas State Seal, over an image of the San Antonio mission.

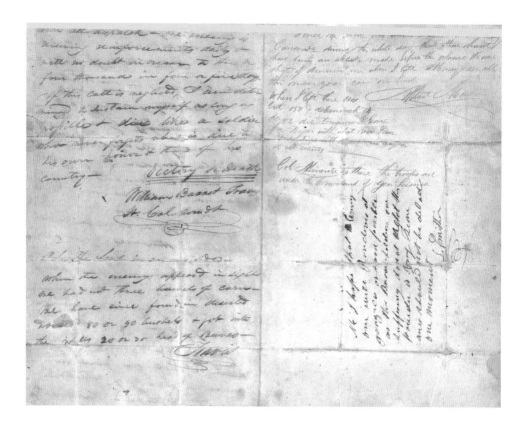

Victory or Death. Lieutenant Colonel William B. Travis's open letter from the Alamo, addressed to "The People of Texas and All Americans in the World."

The Travis letter

Fellow citizens and compatriots

I am besieged, by a thousand or more of the Mexicans under Santa Anna. I have sustained a continual Bombardment and cannonade for 24 hours and have not lost a man. The enemy has demanded a surrender at discretion, otherwise the garrison are to be put to the sword if the fort is taken. I have answered the demand with a cannon shot, and our flag still waves proudly from the walls—I shall never surrender or retreat. Then, I call on you in the name of Liberty, of patriotism and everything dear to the American character, to come to our aid, with all dispatch. The enemy is receiving reinforcements daily and will no doubt increase to three or four thousand in four or five days. If this call is neglected, I am determined to sustain myself as long as possible and die like a soldier who never forgets what is due to his own honor and that of his country—**Victory or Death.**

William Barret Travis
Lt Col comdt

P. S. The Lord is on our side. When the enemy appeared in sight we had not three bushels of corn. We have since found in deserted houses 80 or 90 bushels and got into the walls 20 or 30 head of Beeves.

corpses of the Mexican soldiers he has slain, one of whom has Crockett's long knife buried up to the hilt in his chest.

THE MYSTERY OF THE CHARRED REMAINS

After the battle, Santa Anna ordered the mass cremation of the dead. An eyewitness account of the two huge pyres makes gruesome reading: "In alternate layers the corpses and wood were placed. Grease of different kinds, principally tallow, was melted and poured over the two pyres. They were then ignited and burned until they burned out, leaving but a few fragments of different members. Most of the corpses were entirely consumed."

In 1889, Colonel Seguín stated in a letter that he had salvaged what remains he could from the ashes and buried them beneath the altar of the San Fernando Cathedral in San Antonio—and this appeared to be confirmed when, nearly fifty years later, workmen made an exciting discovery—a rough wooden coffin "moldered into dust, only a few rusty nails survive; a few shreds of military uniforms can still be recognized; a few crushed skulls and charred bones." The remains, immediately assumed to be those of "Travis, Crockett, Bowie, and other Alamo

Heroic remains. *The tomb in San Fernando Cathedral in San Antonio, Texas, alleged to house the remains of Travis, Crockett, Bowie, and the other Alamo heroes.*

"Remember the Alamo!" *Today, the Alamo (pictured below) is the heart of San Antonio and the most visited historic landmark in Texas, ensuring that the heroes who sacrificed their lives are remembered.*

heroes," were entombed on May 11, 1938. However, Seguín's letter contradicts his account on March 28, 1837, of the two smallest heaps of ashes being "carefully collected, placed in a coffin neatly covered with black, and having the names of Travis, Bowie and Crockett, engraved on the inside lid." The coffin was taken in an elaborate procession to the parish church for a funeral, then returned to the spot where they were found and buried. The location was not marked in any way.

This discrepancy, attributed to an error in translation of the 1889 letter, makes it unlikely that the remains in the tomb do include those of American folk hero Davy Crockett. And in any case, as the historian L.W. Kemp observed: "How could any fabric, epaulette or human hair survive such heat that had reduced the bones of one hundred and eighty men to a few fractions?"

ADOLF HITLER

No one dared to enter the room for a few minutes after they heard the shot, although everyone knew exactly what it meant. Hitler had said a formal goodbye to his staff and colleagues an hour earlier, then gone into his study with his new wife and closed the door. When Heinz Linge, his valet, and Martin Bormann, who had served as a witness at his wedding the previous day, finally entered, neither was surprised to see the bodies of the Führer and Eva Braun.

Adolf Hitler
Born: April 20, 1889, Braunau am Inn, Austria
Spouse: Eva Braun (m. April 29, 1945)
Died: April 30, 1945, Berlin, Germany

Eva Anna Paula Braun
Born: February 6, 1912, Munich, Germany
Died: April 30, 1945, Berlin, Germany

ROCHUS MISCH, WHO PLAYED the combined role of courier, bodyguard, and telephone operator in the bunker, would later recall seeing Hitler's corpse slumped, head down on the table, while Braun was curled up on the couch nearby. A strong scent of almonds indicated the presence of cyanide; both had taken capsules, then Hitler, wanting to make absolutely sure, had also shot himself. It was about 3:30pm on April 30, 1945, and Russian troops had already reached the outskirts of Berlin.

THE LAST THREE DAYS

By the closing stages of World War II, Adolf Hitler had been German Chancellor for more than twelve years and the leader of the Nazi party for two decades. By mid-January 1945 he had retreated to his bunker, a claustrophobic series of rooms situated 45 feet/14 meters below the grounds of the Reich Chancellery in Berlin. He made only two public appearances after setting up his center of operations there, and although he refused to accept that the war was lost until around April 20, it was clear to those around him that he was floundering, no longer able to process the military realities that were marking the final defeat of the Reich. One of his secretaries recalled that he alternated between gloomy silences and sudden bursts of often irrational activity, ordering movements of troops that no longer existed, and ranting against those, including Hermann Göring and Heinrich Himmler, who he felt had been disloyal. Once he had accepted the reality of the situation, though, he planned his own end meticulously.

A large quantity of cyanide capsules had been obtained through Himmler and, having taken the decision to die, Hitler ordered that their efficacy be tested by poisoning Blondi, his beloved German Shepherd dog. He no longer trusted Himmler and wanted to be sure that the drugs worked. After the dog's

Architect of the Reich.
Adolf Hitler photographed at his beloved Berghof, the eyrie in the mountains of Bavaria where he spent his leisure time.

death he appeared inconsolable, but rallied through the evening of April 28. He ordered that cyanide capsules be given to all the staff in the bunker so that they, too, could take the suicide option if they wanted. Shortly before midnight he was married to Eva Braun in a short civil ceremony presided over by a local magistrate. Joseph Goebbels and Bormann acted as witnesses and afterward the occupants of the bunker gathered together and drank a champagne toast to the couple. Hitler reminisced about happier times for a while, then, in the early hours, took Traudl Junge, who had worked as one of his secretaries since 1942, into another room and dictated both his will and a political statement that formally expelled Göring and Himmler from the Reich, and appointed Admiral Dönitz as supreme commander of the army and Goebbels as chancellor. By now everyone in the bunker would have been aware that the war was lost; some staff quietly planned escape, while others discussed whether to die at their posts.

The Führer and Eva Braun.
Many of Hitler's intimates despised his mistress, thinking her silly and shallow—but she remained loyal to the bitter end.

Hitler on parade. By *spring 1945, the pageantry that had been so large a part of the Nazi war machine was long over; many senior German officials were beginning to concede that defeat was now inevitable.*

"I NEED 44 GALLONS OF PETROL!"

One of Hitler's fears had been that his body would be put on display to be mocked—news of Mussolini's death, two days earlier, had reached him shortly before and he may also have heard of the indignities heaped on the Italian dictator's corpse. Erich Kempka, Hitler's chauffeur, recalled that he received a panicked telephone call from Otto Günsche, the Führer's adjutant, shortly after the bodies had been discovered. Günsche, was asking for 44 gallons/200 liters of petrol to be delivered to the bunker urgently. "You're mad," Kempka told him, "We don't have those kind of quantities to hand." The whole city was under heavy bombardment and he couldn't reach any of the caches located at certain points around Berlin. Günsche insisted, so Kempka called up his contacts, drained all the official vehicles of fuel and ordered the cans to be taken to the door of the bunker. Entering, he ran into Günsche who revealed that the petrol was needed for "the Chief's" funeral pyre.

"I want to be a beautiful corpse ... I'm going to take poison." —Eva Braun, *the day before her death*

Hitler's body, wrapped in a blanket, was carried up the steps into the Chancellery garden. Martin Bormann followed, carrying the body of Eva Braun. Bombs were exploding all around them, so Kempka, Günsche, Bormann, and Linge dodged in and out of shelter, trying to pour petrol over the bodies and set them alight. Eventually a petrol-soaked rag ignited them and they burned fiercely, the men adding more petrol every time the flames sank down. The fire burned for nearly three hours; a few followers gathered to salute the bodies as they burned but such was the severity of the bombardment that no one stayed long. As soon as they had been reduced to charred bone and ash, the remains were shoveled into a nearby shell crater a few yards away and hastily covered over.

> "I die with a joyful heart in the knowledge … of a contribution unique in the history of our youth which bears my name."
>
> —*Extract from Hitler's last political testament*

April 28, 1945. The Führer gazes out from the door of his bunker at the ruins of the Chancellery. This is believed to be the last picture ever taken of Hitler.

AFTER THE FALL

Between the afternoon of April 30 and the morning of May 2, some of those remaining in the bunker staged a break out and fled. A number committed suicide; in one particularly horrible episode Joseph and Magda Goebbels murdered their six children, then killed themselves. Others were captured, and a few escaped altogether. Meanwhile, on May 1, Admiral Dönitz made a fulsome announcement of Hitler's death "as a hero" on German radio.

Up to this point the accounts of what happened to Hitler and Braun's bodies are broadly similar. But now, they begin to diverge. According to the most common story, by May 2 Russian soldiers were searching the Chancellery. Stalin wanted to know for certain that Hitler was dead (not everyone believed Dönitz's

Hitler's grave? Within just two days of Hitler's death and hasty interment, Russian troops were examining the ruins of the Chancellery. Finding the Führer's body was a priority.

statement, and rumors of the Führer's survival persisted for many years). By the afternoon, the shell crater had been dug over and some remains uncovered. There were ashes, cinders, and, confusing to the Russian soldiers, the remains of one or more dogs (probably those of Blondi and one of her puppies). The remains of Goebbels, his wife, and family were also discovered. The finds were reported to agents of the Russian Army's intelligence agency.

Stalin ordered that the remains be moved, and the most widely accepted account holds that the body fragments, including some teeth and jaw fragments, were taken to Soviet headquarters in Berlin and subjected to a secret autopsy. When the Russians were confident that they had definitely identified the Führer, all the remains were reburied in a forest near the town of Rathenau in June 1945. However, they were dug up again early in 1946 and reburied in the Soviet garrison at Magdeburg, which was to remain the center of Russian activity in Germany for more than two decades.

In 1970, with Magdeburg due to be returned to East Germany, the then-head of the KGB, Yuri Andropov, decided to disinter Hitler one last time. According to the account of one of the KGB officers handed the task, Vladimir Gumenyuk, the team given the job decided to deal with the problem of Hitler's remains once and for all. They took them up into the mountains, burned them once again on an open fire, and scattered the ashes off a cliff. The story was not embellished with any geographical clues. Even this was not quite the end of the saga—Soviet Russia had retained a few pieces of skull which they maintained belonged to Hitler, although on their "rediscovery" in 1993, when tested by a number of forensic experts, most identified them as belonging to a young woman. They may, of course, have belonged to Eva Braun.

The beginning of the end. The front page of the US Army newspaper announcing Hitler's death. On May 7, Germany would sign an unconditional surrender.

LOST AND FOUND

The extraordinary case of medieval English king Richard III, whose body was found in a resolutely twenty-first-century location beneath the gray asphalt of a municipal car park, sparked a resurgence of interest in finding more lost bodies, and the hunt is now on for Alfred the Great. The mortal remains of some individuals have been found only in part, exchanging hands for money and being lodged in ignominious locations—the mummified head of French king Henri IV was stored for years in a box in an attic belonging to a French tax collector. Henri's circumstances haven't improved much since then, as his head is now kept in a Paris bank vault. Other bodies were moved, such as the adored Eva Perón, whose embalmed remains were secretly removed from the country in 1955 after a coup d'état and were believed lost by the Argentinians until she resurfaced to be laid to rest more securely in 1976. Found whole or in part, their stories are convoluted, fascinating, and frequently very surprising.

FORMOSVS·I·PAPA

POPE FORMOSUS

Political intrigue, conflict, and vaulting ambition are all still commonplace in the world today. In 897 they led to the Cadaver Synod in the Basilica St John Lateran, an event so grotesque and gruesome—the clue is in the name—that it is still remembered as a shameful episode in the history of the Roman Catholic Church.

N OT ONLY DID THIS MOST bizarre and shocking affair take place on consecrated ground within the confines of one of the oldest churches in the world, in the holy city of Rome, it was carried out by a pope—the supreme head of the Catholic Church. The victim was also a pope. His birth name is unknown, but he took the papal name of Formosus.

EXCOMMUNICATION

Little is known about the early years of Pope Formosus. His first notable appearance in documented form is in 864 when he was appointed Cardinal Bishop of Porto, a diocese on the coast near Rome. Later he is recorded as having been sent as papal legate to Bulgaria, to settle some doubts entertained by the Bulgarian king on religious matters, and then to France, again on Church business. He began to attract the attention of Pope John VIII, who suspected him of aspiring to become Archbishop of Bulgaria or even of coveting the top job of pope itself. With these accusations lurking in the background, in around 876 Formosus decided it would be prudent to leave Rome and he did so in secret, along with some of the pope's political opponents. John ordered them to return or face excommunication, adding deserting his diocese without permission and performing the divine service despite being forbidden to do so to the list of Formosus's alleged misdeeds.

The exact truth is hard to pin down, but the accusations may have had more to do with Formosus being seen as an opponent to John—Formosus had opposed John's original election to the papacy. John eventually agreed to withdraw his sentence of excommunication providing Formosus promised to stay away from Rome and did not attempt to regain his position as bishop. However, John was assassinated in 882 and was succeeded by Marinus I, who pardoned Formosus and reinstated him as Cardinal Bishop of Porto in 883. After this, he found his influence in the Catholic Church growing steadily and eventually Formosus himself was elected pope in October 891. But Pope John's accusations from earlier in his career would come back to haunt the new pontiff, although by the time they did so it could well have been Formosus doing the haunting.

Pope Formosus. *The victim of a bizarre, posthumous trial. The epitaph on his tomb (now destroyed) read "Formosus, the bishop, distinguished with high praises, pious, frugal, bountiful to the needy, is carried up."*

HELP FROM ABROAD

The already turbulent political climate in Rome now began to heat up even further. Various aristocratic factions were jockeying for position, with Guido, Duke of Spoleto (a region adjacent to lands held by the pope in the Papal States) becoming ever more powerful. Pope Stephen V found himself in the position of having to crown Guido Holy Roman Emperor, possibly unwillingly because the dukes of Spoleto had often been in conflict with the papacy.

Mired in the murk of the history of more than one thousand years ago, the story of what exactly happened next is equally hard to pin down, but the popular view is that opponents of the Spoletan faction decided to appeal for help to the Frankish king, Arnulf of Carinthia (part of modern-day Austria). Now obliged by Guido and his supporters to crown Guido's son, Lambert, co-emperor, Formosus supported this move and sent an embassy to Arnulf. Arnulf responded by

Papal list. *Plaque commemorating the popes buried in St Peter's Basilica in Rome, including Papa Formosus.*

marching into northern Italy in 894. Guido died suddenly in December that year, leaving Lambert sole emperor. Formosus, who wanted to crown Arnulf emperor instead, was imprisoned in the Castel Sant'Angelo, although not for long. By autumn 895, Arnulf was campaigning in Italy again, this time marching south until he stood at the gates of Rome. He entered the city and freed Formosus, who declared Lambert deposed and crowned Arnulf emperor in February 896. So far so good, but unfortunately for Formosus Arnulf then became ill with "paralysis" (possibly a stroke) and had to return to Carinthia. It was at this point that Pope Formosus's eighty-year-old body also jumped ship, and he died on April 4, leaving others to sort out the problem.

Castel Sant'Angelo, Rome. *The castle was built as a mausoleum for Hadrian around 139 CE, and was converted into a fortress in the fifth century. Pope Stephen VI was imprisoned here for several months in 897 before being reputedly strangled.*

THE CADAVER SYNOD

This is where a conventional tale of political machinations takes a surprising and very macabre turn. The exact motivation for what happened next is uncertain, but the commonly held theory is that the Spoletan faction was out for revenge. Lambert encouraged his supporter and the current pope, Stephen VI, to not only dig up the charges that had been made against Formosus by Pope John VIII decades earlier, but also to dig up Formosus himself. The scene that subsequently unfolded at what came to be known as the Cadaver Synod

Holy Roman Emperor

The emperor ruled over the Holy Roman Empire, made up of several different lands in western and central Europe (notably parts of France, Germany, and Italy), which nevertheless retained their own identities and monarchs. The empire, which existed between 800 and 1806, was a significant institution in Europe and the emperor an important figure, normally drawn from the ranks of the Frankish kings; Charlemagne was the first to be crowned.

(also known as Synodus Horrenda) in 897, held within the confines of Rome's Basilica St John Lateran, was horrifying and grotesque in the extreme.

Upon Stephen's orders, the body of Formosus was removed from its tomb around nine months after its interment. The rotting corpse, still dressed in papal vestments, was then propped up on a throne in order that it could suffer the humiliation of a mock trial. The records of the proceedings were later burned, but the accusations hurled at the corpse by Stephen are believed to have included having broken his promise to John VIII by returning to Rome and becoming Bishop of Porto once more, as well as breaking Church law by then becoming pope—at the time it was not permissible for a bishop to move from one holy see to another. But the trial was not entirely convened as a kangaroo court as the deceased Formosus was not without representation—a deacon was appointed to answer for the corpse, and stood by to respond to the charges in what presumably would have been an act of ghoulish ventriloquism.

> "When you were bishop of Porto, why did you usurp the universal Roman See in such a spirit of ambition?"
>
> —*Pope Stephen VI to the corpse of Pope Formosus*

Pope Formosus and Stephen VI (at the Cadaver Synod). As imagined by French artist Jean-Paul Laurens in 1870. Stephen VI points melodramatically at the remains of Formosus as a witness is examined. Incense burning in the thurible in the foreground attempts to control the smell from the corpse.

THE VERDICT

Unsurprisingly Formosus was found guilty, his election as pope was declared invalid as were all the acts that he had carried out in the name of the Church, including the ordination of members of the clergy. The papal vestments were

torn from his body and, as a parting shot, the fingers on his right hand with which he had given priestly blessings were severed. Formosus was then unceremoniously thrown into an ordinary grave. Just a few days later he was dug up again and this time his body was dumped in Rome's River Tiber, to be lost for good.

RIP . . . EVENTUALLY

However, instead of sinking to the bottom of the river, to merge with the mud and to never be seen again, it was retrieved—washing up on the shore where it was rumored to have performed miracles before being spotted and rescued by a monk and reburied in a monastery. Later, one of Stephen's successors, Theodore II, had what was left of Formosus reburied once more, with full papal honors, in St Peter's Basilica, Rome. The verdicts of the synod were themselves annulled and the pontificate of Formosus was declared valid once more, as were all his acts and ordinations … But not for long. A few years later, during the time of Pope Sergius III, part of this reversal was itself reversed. Confusing? Sergius, who had participated in the Cadaver Synod as bishop, reaffirmed its findings, declaring all the appointments within the clergy carried out by Formosus invalid and demanding their reordination, a move that created chaos. For many years it was believed that Sergius (who has not gone down in the annals as a good pope), went even further, having Formosus dug up yet again for another synod, during which the corpse was this time beheaded and thrown into the Tiber yet again, but it proved to be a one freakish story too far and today the body of Formosus lies among those of the medieval popes in St Peter's, intact presumably . . . apart from several fingers on the right hand.

St Peter's Basilica, Rome. *During the demolition of Old St Peter's, which had fallen into disrepair in the early seventeenth century, the tomb of Formosus was destroyed, along with those of many other early popes. The present basilica was consecrated in 1626.*

A high turnover

Pope John VIII was right to have been looking over his shoulder nervously during his time in office. He was the first pope to be assassinated. Although according to some reports an able pope, he evidently couldn't please all the people all the time and a lack of support among those who mattered cost him his life. Despite this, others were waiting in the wings. After Marinus I's short-lived papacy, Adrian III managed barely a year before dying in suspicious circumstances, possibly murdered. Boniface VI was pope for just two weeks, possibly killed on the orders of his successor, Stephen VI, for whom the Cadaver Synod did not prove to be his finest hour. It led to an uprising and Stephen was removed from office a few months later and was thrown into prison where he is said to have been strangled. Romanus, in office for only three or four months in 897, was followed by Theodore II who managed twenty days, again possibly murdered. With the reign of Sergius III began what became known as the Saeculum Obscurum (the Dark Age, nicknamed the Pornocracy) when the Church became even more embroiled in corruption and immorality.

RICARDVS · III · ANG · REX

RICHARD III

As the drill bit into the dull gray tarmac in the unprepossessing setting of a municipal parking lot in the city of Leicester, England, the odds against success were stacked high. The quest? To find the mortal remains of an anointed king, the last Plantagenet and the last English king to die in battle—Richard III.

RICHARD was born in Fotheringhay Castle, in the north of England. His father, also named Richard, was the Third Duke of York, one of the most powerful noblemen in England, and his mother, Cecily Neville, was from a prominent aristocratic family. But even at the unpredictable top table of late medieval England—when kings could be carried off by battle, disease, or a dagger in the night—Richard could not have reasonably expected to become king since he was not in direct line to the throne … so what was the path to kingship?

WARS OF THE ROSES

Richard was born into a period of instability that soon evolved into sporadic conflict over the English throne between the two powerful dynastic houses of Lancaster and York. This would come to be known as the Wars of the Roses (1455–85), but the use of white and red roses as dynastic emblems in the conflict is a later construct—Richard's emblem was a white boar. Nevertheless Yorkist white roses would be strewn across his coffin on its way to his reinterment in Leicester Cathedral more than five hundred years later.

King Henry VI was far removed from his alpha male father Henry V in terms of martial ability and inclination. A kind and pious man but widely regarded as weak, Henry VI was unable to prevent the power struggles that developed during his reign. He also suffered intermittent mental breakdowns during which Richard's father was appointed Lord Protector. It was in 1455, shortly after the king had recovered from just such a breakdown, that the unrest developed into serious conflict. Henry's chief challenger was Richard's father, Third Duke of York. Initially he may have simply wanted to dampen down the Lancastrian influence over the king, but as a descendant of King Edward III's second surviving son, Richard's father now asserted his claim to the throne, which was technically stronger than Henry's (see family tree, p. 82). Margaret of Anjou, Henry VI's wife and queen, took up the baton for the Lancastrians. Richard's father was killed at the Battle of Wakefield in 1460. His eldest son Edward took up the fight for the Yorkists and the Lancastrians were defeated in 1461. Edward was proclaimed King Edward IV and Henry and Margaret fled to Scotland with their only son.

King Richard III. *This portrait in the Royal Collection by an unknown artist dates from the sixteenth century—after Richard's death. He is shown playing with the ring on his little finger, which may symbolize authority or a union, such as marriage.*

LOYALTY BINDS ME

Over the next decade, Edward had to put down several uprisings centered on the old king and was victorious at the decisive Battle of Tewkesbury in 1471, during which Henry's son was killed. The king himself, who was by now imprisoned in the Tower of London, was finally put out of the picture once and for all on May 21 of that year, murdered by an unseen hand.

Richard was a loyal brother to Edward throughout this period and by the time he was in his early twenties, was appearing at court, carrying out public service duties and helping to control the country in the north. Richard married Anne Neville—an advantageous match as she brought with her considerable lands—and as a royal prince, created Duke of Gloucester, he could have expected to lead a comfortable life as one of the most powerful figures in the land. However on April 9, 1483, Edward IV died unexpectedly at the age of 41. He would naturally be succeeded by his son Edward V, but as Edward was still a boy aged 12, Richard (now 31) was appointed Lord Protector, according to the dead king's will.

THE PLOT THICKENS

This is where the story starts to get murky. The Woodvilles, the family of Edward V's mother who had benefited from patronage and titles during his father's reign, possibly fearing reprisals or even that Richard would make a play for the throne now that they no longer had Edward IV's protection, decided that young

Family tree: Primogeniture rules. As a descendant of Edward III's second surviving son, Richard, Third Duke of York's claim to the throne trumped that of Henry VI, a descendant of Edward III's third son.

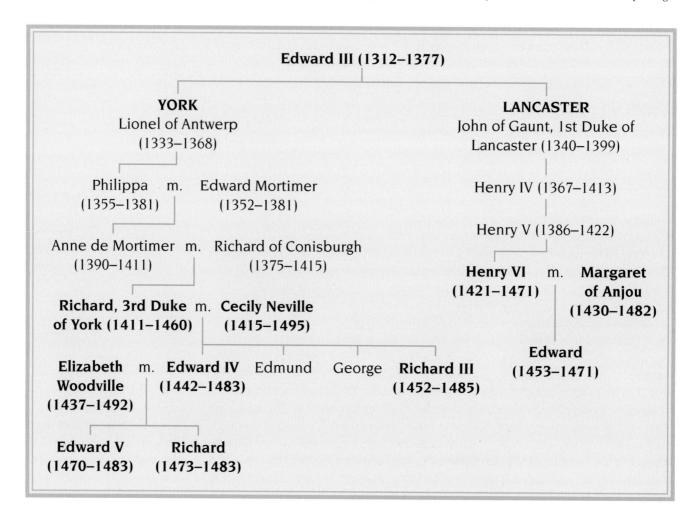

Edward should be crowned at once. They despatched an escort to bring him to London with all haste. However, perhaps concerned that he was going to be squeezed out, Richard intercepted Edward's party en route, took charge of the young prince and escorted him into London, where he was lodged in the Tower (at the time a royal palace as well as a prison). Edward's mother, the dowager queen Elizabeth Woodville, quickly took refuge in Westminster Abbey with her daughters and younger son, also called Richard. Meanwhile Uncle Richard treated Edward with respect and continued with the preparations for the boy's coronation. But on June 13 Richard ordered the execution of several of the Woodvilles' supporters on charges of conspiracy. Next he persuaded Elizabeth Woodville to give up the young Prince Richard on the grounds that he could attend the coronation of his brother. With both young princes now squirreled away in the Tower, Uncle Richard declared his claim to the throne (see panel) and was crowned king on July 6, 1483. The young princes remained in the Tower, but within several weeks they had simply vanished.

RICHARD'S REIGN

Richard's brief reign was marked by personal tragedy when his only son died in 1484, followed by Anne, his queen, in 1485. He had little time in which to make his mark as king, although he instigated a number of reforms of the legal system including the presumption of "innocent until proven guilty" and passed laws that were the first to be published in English rather than Latin or French.

At the end of 1483, soon after his accession, a rebellion in southern England supported by the Woodville family caused trouble for Richard. He put it down but the leaders fled to France where they regrouped around the exiled Henry Tudor, the man who was to prove Richard's nemesis. In 1485, Henry landed in Wales and marched east, challenging Richard's forces at Bosworth on August 22, 1485.

Statue of Richard III outside Leicester Cathedral. *The statue was covered with white roses, emblem of the House of York, on the day of his reinterment, March 26, 2015. Thousands attended the four days of events and ceremonies leading up to his reburial.*

RICHARD'S END

The Battle of Bosworth Field took place in the heart of England, 3 miles/ 5 kilometers west of the city of Leicester. According to the accounts, Richard fought bravely and led a charge of men toward Henry Tudor, but he was famously unhorsed. Polydore Virgil, Henry VII's historian wrote: "King Richard, alone, was killed fighting manfully in the thickest press of his enemies." Richard was outnumbered, on foot, and surrounded by the enemy; blows rained down on him and he was soon cut down, felled by strikes to the head.

After the battle, Richard's body was stripped naked and thrown across a horse to be led into nearby Leicester. It was displayed publicly for three days before being buried inside the Church of Grey Friars in the city, where it lay until 1538 and the dissolution of the monasteries ordered by King Henry VIII. Richard's body would in fact remain there undisturbed for the next five hundred years—it's simply that no one knew that it was there. With the destruction of Grey Friars, the grave's location was lost to history to be replaced by rumors and stories as to what had happened to his remains. One of the more colorful and gruesome was that his corpse had been dug up when the monastery was destroyed, paraded through the streets, and thrown into a river.

CHARACTER ASSASSINATION

There is no doubt that Richard has been the victim of a fairly accomplished character assassination. He appears to have been intelligent, an able administrator, brave, and conventionally pious, but for much of the five hundred years following his death he was portrayed as one of history's bogeymen—a murderer and tyrant. Once the princes had vanished, many a fifteenth-century amateur sleuth quite naturally put two and two together. And it was natural for Richard to have been vilified by his Tudor successors, who would have wanted to put a spin on their own rather dubious obtaining of the throne. A number of prominent people contributed considerably to the blackening of his reputation, including a certain W. Shakespeare of Stratford-upon-Avon, who ensured that the popular image was of evil personified, portraying Richard as a limping hunchback with a withered forearm. A more moderate take on matters would be to assume that the truth of Richard's character lay somewhere in the middle.

DIGGING FOR RICHARD

Although there were many who accepted history's damning verdict on Richard, not everyone believed that the case for him as a total bad guy was quite so cut and dried. And along with the endlessly fascinating "Did he, didn't he?" surrounding the Princes in the Tower was the question of what had happened to his tomb. The most educated of guesses still pointed to Grey Friars, but despite the location of the friary being known—now covered by shops and a parking lot—its precise layout beneath the modern buildings was not.

Here lies a king. Richard's body was buried, presumably hurriedly, in a grave that was too small, without a coffin or a shroud. The hands were crossed at the wrist, possibly because they were still tied. The skeleton revealed that Richard would have had a slender build, but despite the curvature of the spine there was no evidence for a withered arm or a limp.

Deciding to dig in the parking lot was therefore very much a leap of faith, acting on a hunch on the part of Philippa Langley from the Richard III Society, and the chances of finding him were viewed as pretty remote. But work finally began on August 25, 2012, the anniversary of his burial in 1485. A skull was found almost immediately, but the skeleton to which it belonged was not revealed fully until the soil was scraped away a few days later. But then everyone stared in utter disbelief. The skull belonged to a skeleton showing pronounced curvature of the spine (scoliosis). News of the find sped around the world, with some of Richard's supporters who believed the hunchback theory to be simply a rumor spread by his enemies somewhat taken aback by the condition of the spine. The skeleton revealed that the scoliosis would not have produced a hunchback, but rather "unequal shoulders," with the right slightly higher than the left, conforming to contemporary descriptions of him, although clothes and armor would have minimized the effect. There was evidence of eleven wounds on the body, with several to the head including the one that was probably fatal, slicing away part of the base of the skull.

Astonishingly and against all the odds, Richard had been found in the first trench on the first day of the dig. Even better, the trench had been dug close to a letter "R" painted on the tarmac—"R" for Richard and *rex* (king in Latin). Had he wanted to be found? The news was announced officially on February 4, 2013, after the confirmation of a DNA match with two living descendants of his sister.

> "Slightly to my left, on the tarmac, there was something new—a white, hand-painted letter 'R,' denoting a 'reserved' parking spot, but it told me all I needed to know." —*Philippa Langley*

The face of a king. *This facial reconstruction of Richard III, from his skull, bears a striking resemblance to some of his portaits.*

FINAL RESTING PLACE

Richard III was reburied in Leicester Cathedral on March 26, 2015, after several days of ceremonies and events, and television footage was beamed around the world. Inevitably a media affair with all the attendant hullabaloo (celebrity guests, reenactments, television specials), it was nevertheless a significant and historic moment. Although Richard had reputedly been buried "irreverently" in 1485, the friars would have conducted a Roman Catholic funeral service, so the ceremony in 2015 was a reinterment.

The last Plantagenet now lies beneath a simple stone monument bearing his motto "Loyaute me lie"— loyalty binds me—finally at rest in a setting that befits a king.

Richard III Society
Founded in the UK in 1924 as the Fellowship of the White Boar, the society's aim is to reassess and rehabilitate the reputation of the king. The American branch was founded in 1961. "We believe that history has not dealt justly with his posthumous reputation and we aim to encourage and promote a more balanced view."

CERVANTES

In 2015, a team of forensic historians, archaeologists, and anthropologists located a tangle of bones in the long-forgotten crypt beneath the Convent of the Barefoot Trinitarians in Madrid. Among the bones were those of the man dubbed "the father of the modern novel"—Miguel de Cervantes, whose remains had been mislaid not just momentarily, but for more than three centuries.

Miguel de Cervantes
Born: September 29, 1547, Alcalá de Henares, Spain
Spouse: Catalina de Salazar y Palacios (m. 1584)
Children: Isabel de Saavedra (b. 1584) (illegitimate daughter of Cervantes and Ana Franca de Rojas)
Died: April 22, 1616, Madrid
Buried: Madrid

WITHOUT DOUBT, Cervantes is Spain's most celebrated literary export. His novel *Don Quixote*—a tale of knightly chivalry—has been translated into more than 60 languages and has spawned movies, operas, and ballets, a musical, works of art, even a few pop songs. And as with so many great writers, Cervantes's real-life adventures were echoed in his characters and plots.

CERVANTES THE SOLDIER

For much of his life, Cervantes was either getting into trouble or covering himself with glory, and the former often led to the latter. This pattern began when he was a student in Madrid and already showing promise as a writer—one of his sonnets was selected for a book commemorating Queen Elizabeth of Valois, who died in 1568. But the following year a royal warrant was issued for his arrest after he wounded his opponent in a duel. His response was to flee to Rome.

Cervantes joined a Spanish infantry regiment based in Naples in 1570 and shortly after distinguished himself in the Battle of Lepanto on October 7, 1571, where the allied Christian forces of the Holy League, under the command of Don Juan de Austria, defeated the Ottoman Turks. Cervantes was shot twice in the chest and a third time in his left arm, rendering the hand useless. Fortunately for his future literary career, the "one-armed man from Lepanto" was right-handed, and he was philosophical about his injury: "The loss of my left arm is for the greater glory of my right."

SOLD INTO SLAVERY

In 1575, as Cervantes was returning to Spain, his ship was captured by Barbary pirates and he and his brother Rodrigo were sold into slavery in Algiers, the Muslim center of Christian slave traffic. Cervantes was carrying letters of recommendation written by Juan de Austria to his half-brother, King Philip II

A true portrait? There are no authentic contemporary portraits of Cervantes, and his true appearance is unknown. This somewhat haughty interpretation was painted by Juan de Jáuregui twenty years after the author's death.

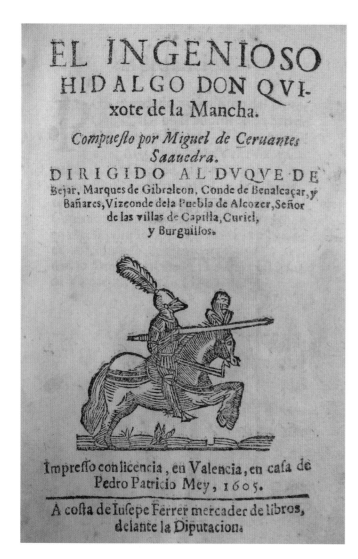

The most celebrated work. *The frontispiece (above left) and a Gustave Doré illustration (above right) from* Don Quixote, *the book that rewarded Cervantes with the sobriquet "The father of the modern novel."*

Cervantes coins a word
The adjective "quixotic," referring to the impractical pursuit of idealistic goals, is derived from *Don Quixote*.

of Spain, which made him a valuable prize—and inflated his ransom price. During his five-year captivity, Cervantes made four daring bids to escape, but was spared the usual punishment of torture, mutilation, or even death—protected, perhaps, by those letters. Here again, he demonstrated courage and leadership among the captive community.

Rodrigo was freed after two years, but Cervantes's family did not raise the requisite sum of 500 gold escudos to secure Miguel's release until 1580. They were assisted by the nuns of Madrid's Convent of the Discalced (Barefoot) Trinitarians, a Catholic religious order founded at the end of the twelfth century for the very purpose of ransoming Christians held captive by nonbelievers. Cervantes was forever grateful to the nuns, to whom he owed his life.

CERVANTES THE CIVIL SERVANT

Returning to Spain, Cervantes found that the glittering future promised by the letters of recommendation failed to materialize. He attempted to launch his literary career, penning a number of plays, of which only two have survived—*The Siege of Numantia* and *Life in Algiers*. In 1585, Cervantes published the first part of a pastoral romance, *La Galatea*; those hoping to read the second part were disappointed, however, because it was never written.

Cervantes was not an immediate hit as a writer and to supplement his income he obtained a post securing provisions for the Invincible Armada, with which Philip II hoped to conquer England. The Armada turned out not to be invincible, and was defeated by the English on July 29, 1588. Cervantes continued in the post, supplying subsequent naval expeditions, and then became a tax collector. Both positions landed him in jail—in 1592, when he was accused of selling wheat without authorization, and again in 1595 when the bank in which he had deposited crown funds went bankrupt. The funds disappeared and Cervantes was blamed. He was found not guilty on both occasions.

THE INGENIOUS GENTLEMAN

In 1605, Cervantes achieved his first major literary success when Part I of his two-part work, *The Ingenious Gentleman Don Quixote of La Mancha*, referred to simply as *Don Quixote*, was published; the lanky eponymous character and his short, chubby squire, Sancho Panza, proved a winning combination and by 1617 the book had been reprinted ten times. Their creator moved back to Madrid and took up residence in the literary quarter now known as the Neighborhood of Letters. Here, he completed the 12 short stories that he began writing in 1590 and published in 1613 as *Exemplary Tales*; he also published *The Journey to Parnassus* (1614) and the second part of *Don Quixote* (1615).

His life now drawing to a close, Cervantes finished his final work, *The Trials of Persiles and Sigismunda*, published posthumously in 1617. "Yesterday I was given last rites," he wrote, "and today I write this: time is short, anxiety grows, hope dwindles and, with all this, I live due to the will I have to live." He died on April 22, 1616, and was buried, in accordance with his will, inside the walls of the Convent of the Barefoot

> "The pen is the language of the soul; as the concepts that in it are generated, such will be its writings." —*Miguel de Cervantes*

Within these walls. *The Convent of the Discalced (Barefoot) Trinitarians in Madrid. A stone plaque commemorates Cervantes's rescue and his wish to be buried within its walls.*

Trinitarians. And there, less than fifty years later, we lose track of him. His remains were temporarily housed at another convent while the Trinitarians' convent was being rebuilt, and were then returned and reburied—but where?

THE SEARCH BEGINS

In April 2014, reports indicated that forensic archaeologists were to use special equipment to try to locate Cervantes's remains in the convent, declared a Property of Cultural Interest in 1943 and still home to a few elderly nuns. The estimated cost of the operation, focused on the oldest part of the building, was 100,000 euros (around $110,000)—a modest sum, given the world's admiration for the author. Raising the money proved challenging, however, and by the time the project received the green light, there was an element of urgency—plans were in place to celebrate the 400th anniversary of Cervantes's death in 2016 and unearthing his remains just in time would be a triumph. But it was not an exercise to be rushed. The historian Fernando de Prado said that locating the burial place would be the easy part; exhuming the bones and identifying those of Cervantes would be a far more delicate operation, although the wounds he received at Lepanto would have left a useful imprint. Also, only around fifteen people were buried with Cervantes at the convent, which at the time of his death was one of the "smallest, poorest, and most abandoned," and the chances of more than one of those being a male aged around 70 at death, with an incapacitated left hand and a bullet wound in the chest, were remote.

Scanning for the crypt. *Forensic archaeologists set to work to locate the remains of Cervantes in the ornate Convent Church. The scanning equipment helped pinpoint the site of the crypt.*

CERVANTES RESURFACES

On January 29, 2015, a disintegrated casket was found in an alcove in the crypt, along with the remains of several other bodies. On one of the casket fragments were the initials "MC," picked out in tacks. The researchers were only cautiously excited, however—the real proof would still depend on examination of the bones. Less than two months later, the news broke: "He's there. We know that some of these bones belong to Cervantes." None of the bones bore evidence of wounds sustained at Lepanto, however; the conclusion was based instead on historical and archaeological evidence—the age of the bones and remnants of clothing.

The forensic anthropologist Francisco Etxeberria remarked that the search itself had become an informal tribute to the author, and that alone had made it worthwhile. "And now on top of that we actually found something," he added. Cervantes was buried in the convent—again—on June 11, 2015, with military honors. And the only thing that's missing? Definitive proof that the bones reburied in the convent do belong to Cervantes …

Fragments of Cervantes?
These bone fragments are believed to belong to Cervantes. There are no known family members, living or dead, with whom to compare the DNA.

Shared anniversary
Cervantes died within a few days of another literary giant—none other than Shakespeare. Festivals celebrating "Shakespeare y Cervantes" were held in several countries in 2016, a joint venture organized by the Hay Festival (a British annual literature festival), Acción Cultural Española (the Spanish cultural agency), and the British Council.

HENRI IV

Henri IV, or Henri le Grand, known affectionately by his subjects as Good King Henri, was one of France's best-loved kings—but sadly, this did not guarantee him eternal rest. He was assassinated by a Catholic fanatic. Nearly two hundred years later, his skeleton was rudely disinterred by revolutionaries and decapitated; and now a mummified head claimed to belong to Henri is still causing some dissension.

Henri of Navarre, king of France
Born: December 13, 1553, Pau, France
Reigned: 1572–1610
Spouse: Margaret of Valois (m. 1572); Marie de' Medici (m. 1600)
Children: Louis XIII (b. 1601), Elisabeth (b. 1602), Christine (b. 1606), Nicolas Henri (b. 1607), Gaston (b. 1608), Henrietta Maria (b. 1609)
Died: May 14, 1610, Paris, France

HENRI WAS BORN to the future king and queen of Navarre, a small Basque kingdom straddling land in present-day Spain and France. His parents were of different faiths: His father, Antoine, was a Catholic, while his mother, Jeanne, was a Huguenot and the acknowledged spiritual and political leader of the French Protestant movement. She was a key figure in the early Wars of Religion, fought between Catholics and Protestants in France from 1562 to 1598—which it fell to her son, Henri, to resolve.

PARIS IS WORTH A MASS

While Protestantism was replacing Catholicism in many northern European countries in the sixteenth century, people in France remained staunchly Catholic, with the exception of those inspired by the theologian John Calvin, whose catechism for French Protestants, *Institutes of the Christian Religion*, was published in 1536. These Protestants became known as Huguenots.

Although Henri was baptized a Catholic, his mother raised him in the Protestant faith after his father died in 1562. On August 5, 1570, the Peace of Saint-Germain ended the third of the nine bitter Wars of Religion, and to cement

Henri's work is undone
King Louis XIV, Henri's grandson, celebrated as "Louis the Great" and "the Sun King," reigned from 1643 to 1715: He was persuaded by his advisors that the Huguenots were a threat to the absolute authority of the monarch, and gradually their privileges were eroded. In 1685, Louis revoked the Edict of Nantes and many Huguenots left France to seek refuge in Protestant countries, including England—thus introducing the word "refugee" into the English language.

Henri IV, the first Bourbon king of France. A *portrait of "Le Vert Galant"* ("the gay old spark") as Henri was fondly dubbed because of his tendency to enjoy amorous adventures.

the uneasy truce between the two sides, Jeanne arranged the marriage of Henri to Margaret, the Catholic sister of the French king, Charles IX. The marriage took place in August 1572, shortly after Jeanne's death in June of that year—so mercifully she was not to experience the St Bartholomew's Day massacre of Protestants gathered in Paris for the event, when so many were killed in the streets that the River Seine ran red with their blood. The massacre spread throughout France and in total around ten thousand Huguenots were murdered.

On Jeanne's death, Henri inherited the monarchy of Navarre and in 1584 he also became heir presumptive to the throne of France. He acceded in 1589, but not until the eighth War of Religion—known as the War of the Three Henrys because the chief protagonists were all named Henri—had been fought. The ninth and final war—during which Henri IV converted back to Catholicism, responding to a cry that "Paris is worth a Mass"—ended in April 1598 with the Edict of Nantes, which confirmed Catholicism as the state religion but granted the Protestants substantial rights. Everyone was happy; everyone loved Henri.

> "If God gives me life, I will ensure there is no laborer in my kingdom who has not the means to have a chicken in his pot each Sunday!" —*Henri of Navarre*

A PEACEFUL REIGN

Having astutely ended the religious conflict, Henri set to work to return France to a state of prosperity, surrounding himself with ministers with whom he shared a mutual trust. He brought an end to a long war with Spain; he lowered taxes; he restored France's alliance with the Ottoman Empire, which had faltered during the Wars of Religion; and opened up trade routes to East Asia. Henri was a king who cared about his people, using kindness rather than force—although he was also rather too fond of chasing women.

A future king. A *Delacroix painting depicting Henri IV conferring the regency on Marie de Médicis on behalf of their son, Louis XIII, who was only 8 years old when Henri was assassinated.*

Despite all this, it turned out that Henri was not, after all, loved by absolutely everyone—some Catholics considered him, as an erstwhile Protestant, to have usurped the throne, while some Protestants considered him a traitor for reverting to Catholicism. He survived several assassination attempts but was stabbed to death in Paris by François Ravaillac, a Catholic fanatic, on May 14, 1610. Good King Henri was no more, and he was buried in the Basilica of Saint-Denis.

Henri meets his end. A *victim of the religious fanaticism he was striving to eradicate, Henri is assassinated when the Catholic François Ravaillac rushes at him wielding a knife.*

HENRI LOSES HIS HEAD

Just over one hundred and eighty years later, battles over succession to the throne became irrelevant when Louis XVI fell victim to the French Revolution. The monarchy was abolished on September 21, 1792, and Louis was executed four months later. Not satisfied with merely putting the country's aristocracy and their supporters to the guillotine while the *tricoteuses* looked on, animatedly knitting the *bonnets rouges*—red liberty caps—that came to symbolize the uprising, the revolutionaries also ransacked the royal chapel at Saint-Denis. Long-dead monarchs, including Good King Henri, were roused from their eternal slumber, mutilated, and tossed carelessly into mass graves. But someone was seen rescuing a severed head from the confusion, and when the graves were opened in 1817 during a short-lived restoration of the Bourbon monarchs (of whom Henri had been the first), it was Henri's head that was missing …

HEAD IN A BOX

For two centuries, a mummified head said to be Henri's changed hands constantly—auctioned, held in a private collection for a while, auctioned again. In 1919, a photographer named Joseph-Émile Bourdais won the head at auction for the sum—not even princely, let alone kingly—of three francs. He dedicated much of his life to establishing its authenticity, without success. He died in 1946, and in 1953 a retired tax collector, Jacques Bellanger, a resident of Angers in western France, purchased a head—presumably the same one—and stored it in a discarded wardrobe in his attic, wrapped in an old towel and placed in a box.

MYSTERY SOLVED . . .

In 2008, M. Bellanger unwrapped the head with a flourish to show to Stéphane Gabet, coauthor of the book *Henri IV: The Mystery of a Headless King*: "The mummified head appeared, well conserved, impressive. It was a magic moment."

Two years later, scientists declared that the head—still with its brain, which had shrunk to the size of a walnut—was indeed that of Henri. Their conclusion was based on a digital facial reconstruction, based upon 3D scans of the skull, which also matched contemporary portraits, together with radiocarbon dating that showed the age of the head matched Henri's date of death, along with X-rays.

The discovery was made even more exciting when, in 2013, it was reported that DNA from the skull had been compared with that taken from a blood-stained handkerchief stored in a gourd elaborately decorated with heroes of the French Revolution—a grisly memento of the execution of none other than Louis XVI—and a shared rare genetic signature had been revealed. There could not have been a more relevant pairing for a "belt-and-suspenders" confirmation. "The DNA is clear," stated Gabet's coauthor, Philippe Charlier, triumphantly. So surely the moment had come to return King Henri's head to its rightful place in the Basilica of Saint-Denis, with the solemn funeral ceremony he deserved?

. . . BUT UNRESOLVED

Unfortunately, it is not that simple. The discovery has sparked something of a dynastic disagreement between two of the pretenders to the long defunct French throne. Henri d'Orléans, Count of Paris and Duke of France, is not at all convinced about the validity of the outcome. "What are we supposed to see from this supposed facial reconstitution," he demands scathingly, "that he had a Bourbon nose?" Prince Louis de Bourbon, Duke of Anjou, on the other hand, thinks it's time to reunite Henri's head with his body.

Royal necropolis. *The Basilica of Saint-Denis to the north of Paris, dubbed "the royal necropolis of France" as the remains of all but three French monarchs from the tenth century to 1789 lie here.*

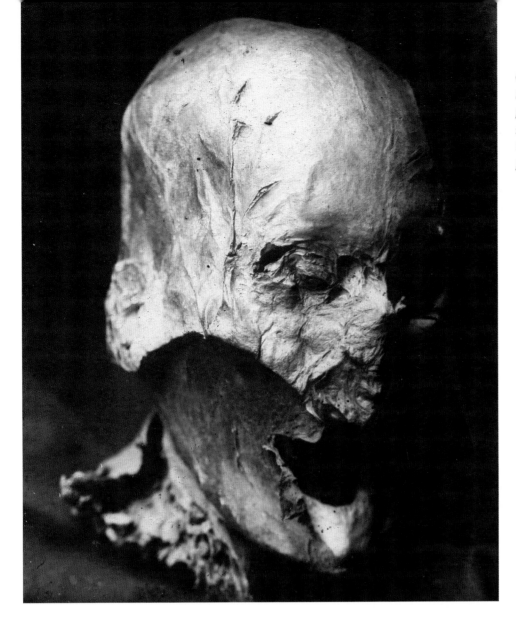

Gruesome relic. *The mummified head that changed hands frequently for two centuries and is currently stored in a Paris bank vault until the argument over its origin is finally settled.*

And there is another problem—a second test comparing DNA from the skull and the blood on the handkerchief with DNA of three living Bourbon descendants negated the findings of the first test, and it was suggested that both the skull and the blood could have belonged to totally unimportant people. It seems that ancient DNA is typically degraded, and establishing accurate genetic sequences is more likely to take decades than weeks. Cross-contamination is also likely to cloud the results. According to Jean-Jacques Cassiman, the geneticist who made the latest claim, "The owner of the head does not appear related to the owner of the blood nor to the living Bourbons through either maternal or paternal lines."

"The nose was broken and bent to the left ... the head was a brownish colour, with the mouth wide open ... Almost all the soft tissue remained." *—Description of the skull*

As it stands, then, Dr Olivier Pascal, President of the French Institute of Genetic Testing, says there is still no conclusive proof and that the information would not stand up in a court of law. So for the moment at least, the head presumed to be Henri's continues to languish in the undignified setting of a Paris bank vault, hoping one day to be awarded a decent burial.

OLIVER CROMWELL

Between 830 CE and the present day, England has been without a monarch for only eleven years—the period in the middle of the seventeenth century when Parliament beheaded King Charles I and the country was ruled by Oliver Cromwell. But the Royalists exacted their revenge when the monarchy was restored and Cromwell, in his turn, lost his head—posthumously.

Oliver Cromwell
Born: April 25, 1599, Huntingdon, England
Spouse: Elizabeth Bourchier (m. 1620)
Children: Robert (b. 1621), Oliver (b. 1622), Bridget (b. 1624), Richard (b. 1626), Henry (b. 1628), Elizabeth (b. 1629), James (b. 1632), Mary (b. 1637), Frances (b. 1638)
Died: September 3, 1658, Whitehall Palace, London
Buried: Westminster Abbey; Tyburn Gallows; Sidney Sussex College

OLIVER CROMWELL WAS BORN into a wealthy family of landed gentry. He attended Sidney Sussex, a Cambridge University college founded in 1596 with a strict Puritan ethos, but it was not until Cromwell experienced a profound spiritual awakening some years later that he wholeheartedly embraced Puritanism. He would return to his old college many years later, under very unusual circumstances.

CROMWELL, THE CHURCH, AND PARLIAMENT

Oliver Cromwell was indirectly related to an equally famous character—Thomas Cromwell, whose sister Katherine married Oliver's great-great-grandfather. Thomas rose rapidly from obscurity to become Earl of Essex and principal advisor to Henry VIII. He was the key figure in the Reformation of the Church in England from Roman Catholic to Protestant, and in the subsequent dissolution of the monasteries. In fact, it was Thomas who helped Oliver's family acquire the substantial areas of former monastic land they owned in East Anglia. Thomas also instituted a number of governmental reforms, heralding the system of parliamentary control that would be fostered by his descendant Oliver more than one hundred years later.

Oliver Cromwell began his political career in 1628, when he became Member of Parliament (MP) for Huntingdon, a small town in the east of England. It was a turbulent time to enter politics. England had had a parliament since 1215, when King John signed the Magna Carta, the charter of liberties upon which the United States' 1791 Bill of Rights and the 1948 Universal Declaration of Human Rights are based. The terms of the charter included the right of the English barons to advise the king. By the end of the fourteenth century, Parliament consisted of two houses, the Upper House (the Lords) and the Commons.

When Charles I ascended the throne in 1625, however, he decided he could manage without the advice or consent of Parliament and instead rely solely on royal prerogative. Parliament, of course, disagreed. The stirrings of dissension came to a head on March 10, 1629, when Charles dissolved Parliament. He did

Portrait of a tyrant. *Oliver Cromwell by Robert Walker, c. 1649, the year in which he signed Charles I's death warrant.*

not summon another until 1640, and only then because he had no choice—he needed money to settle the Bishops' Wars with Scotland, a conflict over his introduction of the 1637 Book of Common Prayer, which contained a traditional liturgy—effectively a reintroduction of Catholicism, and contrary to the austerity of Scottish Presbyterian worship. Cromwell's sympathies were with the Scots; by now, his commitment to Puritanism was deep and uncompromising, to the extent that he advocated abolishing the episcopate, together with the High Church ritual over which the bishops presided. As an adversary for Charles I, Cromwell was the perfect fit.

> "It is high time for me to put an end to your sitting in this place ... ye are a factious crew, and enemies to all good government." —Oliver Cromwell

THE ENGLISH CIVIL WAR

The first parliament summoned by Charles in 1640 failed almost immediately; the MPs were nursing grievances and not in the mood to accommodate his request for funds. The Scots then invaded England again, and the crippling terms of the peace treaty obliged Charles to call a second parliament, known as the Long Parliament, which seized the opportunity to dismantle Charles's policy of Personal Rule. Acts were passed that disempowered the king and did nothing to improve the relationship between Parliament and Charles, who summoned his supporters and on August 22, 1642, raised the royal standard, signaling the start of the English Civil War.

CHARLES LOSES THE BATTLE

It was now that Cromwell showed his true mettle. He proved a shrewd, talented, and successful military leader, despite having no military training or experience before the outbreak of the war, and masterminded the creation in February 1645 of the powerful Parliamentarian New Model Army. On June 14, the fifteen

The execution of Charles I. *The king stepped out of an upstairs window of the Whitehall Palace Banqueting House, London, onto the scaffolding erected for the occasion, with iron staples for securing ropes should the prisoner resist his fate.*

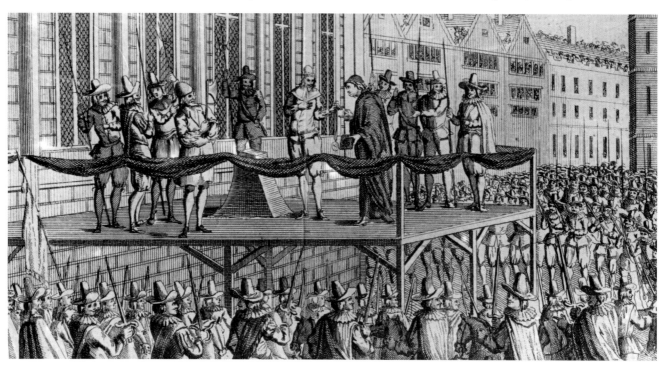

thousand-strong army defeated a much smaller Royalist army at Naseby and effectively won the war. Charles fought on, but in 1649 Parliament tried him for waging war against his kingdom. Unsurprisingly, he was found guilty, and Cromwell signed his death warrant. The king was executed on a scaffolding platform outside Whitehall Palace.

KING IN ALL BUT NAME

In January 1651, Charles's son was crowned Charles II of Scotland. Later that year, he invaded England with a Scottish army, only to be defeated on September 3 in the Battle of Worcester, which finally ended the Civil War. Charles fled into exile. Cromwell, meanwhile, ruled the so-called Commonwealth through the Rump Parliament, consisting of the MPs who had ordered the king's trial. By 1653, however, he'd had quite enough of their obstruction of his efforts to establish a republican government. He delivered an impassioned speech, peremptorily abolished Parliament, and appointed himself Lord Protector of England, Scotland, and Ireland, with a new Parliament made up solely of his supporters. In 1657, Parliament offered him the title of king, but he declined.

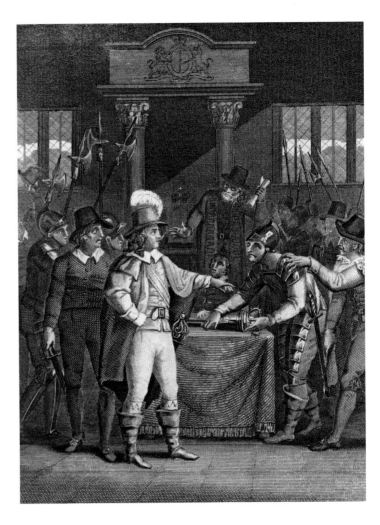

Dissolution of the Long Parliament, 1653. *The king demanded of his Members of Parliament: "Is there a single virtue now remaining amongst you? Is there one vice you do not possess?"*

CROMWELL'S END

After a remarkable career, during which he was both admired for his military prowess and despised for murderous anti-Catholic campaigns in Ireland, Cromwell met a rather unremarkable death. In September 1658, at the age of 59, he succumbed to grief over the death of his favorite daughter and to a recurrent infection and died at Whitehall Palace.

Cromwell was given a regal send-off. A wooden effigy sporting his death mask was displayed for his mourners. It held an orb and scepter, while above the head was a crown on a velvet cushion. His body had been buried a few days earlier in

---

Killjoy Cromwell

Life in Cromwell's England was cheerless. He was particularly adamant that no one should engage in frivolous activities on a Sunday, and feasting on saints' days and the joyous celebration of Christmas were prohibited. Theaters and inns were closed, sports were banned, and punishments for transgressions ranged from whipping to fines to imprisonment. However, Cromwell himself was exempt; he enjoyed hunting and music, and guests at his daughter's wedding at Whitehall Palace were entertained by 48 violinists, 50 trumpeters, and dancing until dawn.

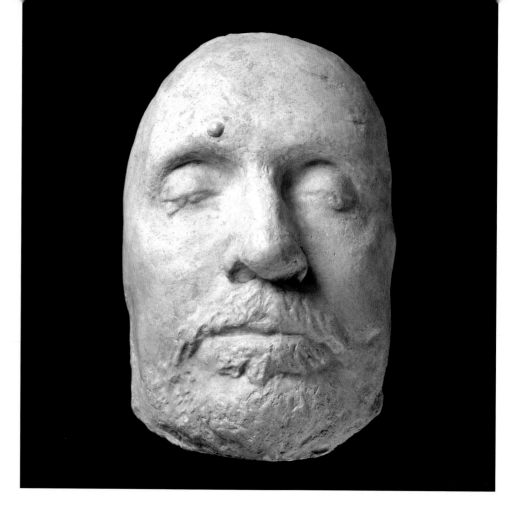

Warts and all. Cromwell suffered from facial warts, as can be seen from his death mask. But he abhorred personal vanity and is said to have insisted that his portrait was painted with "all these roughnesses, warts and everything as you see me."

Westminster Abbey without ceremony, in accordance with his religious principles, but his effigy enjoyed an elaborate procession to the abbey for a state funeral service. Cromwell's story should have ended there—but it did not.

ROYALIST REVENGE

Cromwell was succeeded briefly and unsuccessfully as Lord Protector by his son Richard, and with the Commonwealth in disarray and another civil war threatening, a new Parliament negotiated the restoration of the monarchy. Charles II returned from exile, but before his coronation took place the gleeful Royalists ordered the exhumation of Cromwell's body, which was dragged to Tyburn gallows and publicly hanged, then beheaded for good measure—on January 30, 1661, the 12th anniversary of Charles I's execution.

His corpse was thrown into an unmarked pit at Tyburn, near Marble Arch, where it presumably still rests, beneath paving or tarmac and driven or walked over by modern Londoners thousands of times a day. His severed head was impaled on a traitor's pole on the roof of Westminster Hall, along with the heads of two cosignatories of Charles's death warrant—a vivid warning not to mess with

Charles I, lost and found
After his execution, there was some confusion over the location of Charles I's body. It was eventually discovered in 1813, in a plain casket in Henry VIII's tomb in the royal vault at Windsor Castle. The decomposing head was, of course, separate from the body, but still bore Charles's distinctive "Van Dyck" beard.

Revenge: A dish best served cold. *Cromwell is belatedly hanged (left) and his severed head impaled on a pole (below).*

the monarch. Here the shriveled heads remained, in all winds and weathers, for more than twenty years, until the pole bearing Cromwell's head snapped and its macabre finial rolled into a gutter.

THE TRAVELING HEAD

A sentry collected and secretly guarded the head until his death, when his daughter sold it. It was then ghoulishly displayed by an assortment of showmen, before being purchased in 1841 by a more respectful owner. In 1934, the custodian of the moment, Canon Horace Wilkinson, allowed a detailed medical examination of the head, which confirmed it as "probably or certainly" Cromwell's, and on March 25, 1960, the unwittingly itinerant head finally found rest—in a secret location within the chapel of Cromwell's old college, Sidney Sussex, Cambridge.

Sidney Sussex College, *University of Cambridge, England—Cromwell's alma mater, where his head finally found rest around three hundred years after his death.*

MOZART

To be born with exceptional musical ability is a rare gift. To exhibit that gift as a child prodigy is even more remarkable—but the Austrian composer Mozart did exactly that, embarking on his first European tour at the age of seven. How could so great an artist end up sharing a paupers' grave, and then get lost altogether?

Wolfgang Amadeus Mozart
Born: January 27, 1756, Salzburg, Austria
Spouse: Constanze Weber (m. 1782)
Children: Raimund (b. 1783), Karl (b. 1784), Johann (b. 1786), Theresia (b. 1787), Anna Maria (b. 1789), Franz (b. 1791)
Died: December 5, 1791, Vienna, Austria
Buried: St Marx Cemetery, Vienna, Austria

MOZART WAS ONE OF THREE famous Classical composers known collectively as the First Viennese School. Yet despite being widely acclaimed in his day, and creating an extraordinary repertoire in musical genres from piano concertos to opera, Mozart did not die a wealthy man. His penury at the time of his death spawned much retrospective speculation about his burial, which to the modern eye appears to have been in a paupers' grave.

A LIFE IN MUSIC

Mozart's father, Leopold, was himself a composer, violinist, and teacher. He was quick to recognize the budding talents of his daughter, Maria Anna, and her younger brother, Wolfgang, who were to become known as the "Wunderkinder"— wonder children. Leopold taught them to play the piano and the violin, little Wolfgang mastering both instruments by the age of four, when he also composed his first piano concerto. In 1762, Leopold took the children to Vienna, where they performed for the imperial family. It was just the start—between 1763 and 1768 they took Europe by storm, entertaining exalted audiences including King Louis XV and his mistress, Madame de Pompadour, in Paris and King George III and Queen Charlotte in London, where Mozart composed his first two symphonies.

In 1770, Mozart traveled to Italy with his father; Maria Anna had by now given up performing, considered an unseemly activity for a woman. The tour was a great success, and Mozart received his first commission for an opera, *Mitridate, Re di Ponto*—or at least his first official commission; he had already written *La Finta Semplice*, a three-act comic opera, two years earlier, at the age of 12, at the suggestion of Holy Roman Emperor Joseph II. Back in Salzburg and now aged 18, Mozart was appointed provost of the city's court orchestra, although he continued to tour and accept commissions, much to the annoyance of his employer, Prince-Archbishop Colloredo. In Vienna, he met Haydn—the third composer, together with Beethoven and Mozart, of the First

"It is a mistake to think that the practice of my art has become easy to me." —*Wolfgang Amadeus Mozart*

The Boy Mozart, *painted in 1763. His miniature court dress was a gift from the imperial court in Vienna.*

The boy becomes a man. *Mozart as an adult. The charmed life he led as a child prodigy gave way to a more difficult existence, as he struggled to balance his creativity with bouts of depression.*

Viennese School—and Salieri, whose position as imperial court composer Mozart coveted and finally attained in 1787.

In 1781, Mozart wrote the opera *The Abduction from the Seraglio*. The heroine of the piece was called Constanze, and was based on the love of Mozart's life, Constanze Weber, who also came from a musical family. The couple were married in 1782. "I love her and she loves me with all her heart," he wrote to his disapproving father. "Tell me whether I could wish for a better wife." And indeed he could not—Constanze was to become his inspiration. He composed copiously, and only one thing marred the happiness of their marriage—the death at birth, or shortly afterward, of four of their six children.

REQUIEM

After his marriage, Mozart produced some of his best works. Between 1784 and 1786 he composed nine piano concertos, as well as the comic opera *The Marriage of Figaro*, closely followed in 1787 by *Don Giovanni*. Now hurtling inexorably toward his death, his output became even more prolific, including *Eine Kleine Nachtmusik* and *Cosí fan Tutte*. By 1791, he was frantically busy, working on *The Magic Flute* as well as a coronation opera for Leopold II, king of Bohemia.

Mozart also began to compose a *Requiem*—his own, as it turned out, although it was actually commissioned by an anonymous patron. His health was deteriorating rapidly; a sufferer of rheumatism, he was in great pain, and convinced he was being poisoned. Perhaps he was right—the 1979 play (and 1984 movie) *Amadeus* offers a compelling case for Mozart's colleague Salieri being the perpetrator, and indeed the elderly Salieri was reported to claim in moments of senility that he had poisoned Mozart, although when lucid he hotly denied any such thing. Either way, Mozart enjoyed one last triumph when *The Magic Flute* premiered to great acclaim, but died, depressed, delusional, and burnt out, shortly before his 36th birthday.

Requiem for a great composer. *Mozart on his deathbed, composing his famous Requiem with Constanze at his side. The last words he set to music were "that day of tears and mourning" from the "Lacrimosa."*

MOZART AND MONEY

When it came to managing money, Mozart was a disaster. His reputation as a musical genius grew throughout his teenage years but at the age of 20 he was still in his poorly paid court position. When Colloredo grew exasperated with his long absences, Mozart resigned, and there followed a dark period, both financially and creatively. Mozart the insignificant-looking adult was nowhere near as appealing as Mozart the charming child prodigy, and no one was interested in him; he was reduced to taking students and composed very little. Once married to Constanze, the creative tide turned; money, however, would ebb and flow constantly for the rest of his life.

A PAUPERS' GRAVE?

It so happened that at the time of Mozart's death, the family coffers were all but empty. A committed hedonist, both Mozart and Constanze enjoyed a highly extravagant lifestyle, even in lean times; also, Constanze was often in poor health, necessitating costly treatment. As the years passed, Mozart battled fruitlessly to conquer their financial difficulties.

A monument to Mozart. *Located in the Imperial Palace Gardens, Vienna, the monument was built in 1896 by the Austrian sculptor Viktor Tilgner, who died of a heart attack the day after completing it.*

What happened to Mozart after his death seems a reflection of his impecunious state. Following a perfunctory memorial service in St Stephen's Cathedral, Vienna, his corpse was taken in its cheap coffin to St Marx Cemetery and placed in a grave with five other bodies. There was no cortege, and the body was interred wrapped in linen—the coffin served only as transportation. Even the exact location of the grave is unknown; today, sculptor Florian Josephu-Drouot's "Mourning Genius" marks the spot, based on guesswork.

And it gets worse—after a mere ten years or so of resting in peace, the skeletons in his shared grave were evicted and the space filled with a new batch of temporary occupants. The Mozarteum Foundation in Salzburg possesses a skull alleged to be Mozart's, but DNA analysis has failed to confirm this. Mozart's remains could, in effect, be anywhere.

Happy birthday, dear Mozart

In truth, Mozart was not thrown into a paupers' mass grave; he was merely buried in accordance with the austere funerary regulations of the time. And any perceived lack of a proper show of respect on his death was redressed on the 250th anniversary of his birth in 2006, when exuberant celebrations were held around the world.

THE ROMANOVS

The story of the last days of the Romanov family, set against the turbulent backdrop of the Russian Revolution, has entered legend. The Romanov dynasty had ruled Russia from 1613 but when the eighteenth emperor, Nicholas II, ascended the throne in 1894, he could not have conceived that his would be the last head to wear the imperial crown, nor that his life and that of his entire immediate family would end in tragedy.

B Y THEIR NATURE massacres are messy, and the murder of the last tsar was no exception. The cellar in which it happened measured just 25 by 21 feet/ 7.5 by 6.5 meters, and with eleven victims—and nearly the same number of assassins—it was crowded. Those who planned it had not allowed for the deafening effects of the noise once the shooting started, and some of the killers had had to drink heavily to get up their nerve. But when the deed was done, Tsar Nicholas II, his wife, their five children, three of their servants, and the family's doctor lay dead. What happened afterward, though, was to become a matter of hearsay and conjecture for more than seventy years.

Tsar Nicholas II
Born: Tsarskoye Selo, May 18, 1868

Tsarina Alexandra Feodorovna, née Princess Alix of Hesse
Born: Darmstadt, June 6, 1872

Their children:
Grand Duchess Olga, (b. November 15, 1895)
Grand Duchess Tatiana (b. June 10, 1897)
Grand Duchess Maria (b. June 26, 1899)
Grand Duchess Anastasia (b. June 18, 1901)
Tsarevich Alexei (b. August 12, 1904)

Death: All murdered at Ipatiev House, Ekaterinburg, July 17, 1918

AFTER ABDICATION

In March 1917, after riots had broken out in St Petersburg and the government had resigned following a decade of simmering revolutionary unrest, Nicholas II was forced to abdicate. He immediately rejoined his family at the Alexander Palace at Tsarskoe Selo, the imperial family's home outside the city. There had been no detailed planning for what happened next, but a request was made for the family to go to England, with talk of them taking up temporary residence at Balmoral, the Scottish estate of the British royal family. Shamefully, George V dithered—in the middle of the long and expensive World War I and at a time when the royal families of Europe were becoming fearful of popular opinion, he was unsure whether offering sanctuary to his Russian cousin would be wise. In any case, it was probably too late: With discussions ongoing, all four of the young grand duchesses came down with a severe case of the measles and by the time they were starting to recover, the die was cast and the opportunity for escape lost.

As the summer dragged on, the new government, led by the moderate Alexander Kerensky, moved the family to the Governor's House in Tobolsk, in Siberia. Life was still relatively comfortable, although not free: Their household traveled with them, and lessons with their two tutors, the Swiss Pierre Gilliard and

The Russian imperial family. *Photographed c.1913, this serene image belies the Romanovs' unpopularity. In particular, the empress was pilloried for her close friendship with "the mad monk," the healer Grigoriy Rasputin.*

the Englishman Sydney Gibbes, continued as normal for the younger children. Christmas 1917 offered homemade entertainment, with amateur theatricals, two Christmas trees—one for the family and another for the guards—and plenty of post and parcels from absent family and friends. The guards were friendly, by and large, and many were touched by the family's plight—in particular that of the lively, pretty girls.

To the west, however, Kerensky's government had already fallen in the October Revolution. Lenin, infinitely more radical, was struggling to consolidate his government and was all too aware that Nicholas and his family would be a focus of interest. Personally, he felt that the ex-tsar should be put on trial, but accepted that this might be hard to arrange. After discussions with Yakov Sverdlov, Soviet Communist Party secretary and Lenin's right-hand man, it was proposed that the family be quietly moved to Ekaterinburg, a Bolshevik stronghold in the Urals, where they could be held until the next step became evident.

"THE BAGGAGE"

By February 1918, it had become clear to Nicholas, Alexandra, and their children that things were changing. The friendly, informal guards had mostly been replaced by less affable, grimmer characters. In April, Vasily Yakovlev, one of Sverdlov's

One of the last photographs taken of Nicholas. *The 50-year-old tsar had aged visibly during the final year of his reign. His guards are visible in the background.*

trusted assistants, arrived at Tobolsk with a so-called "Special Purpose Detachment" of one hundred and fifty Red Guards. On April 26, the family were split up: Nicholas, Alexandra, and Maria were sent by train to Ekaterinburg, while Alexei (who was very ill, having suffered a haemophiliac flare-up) and the other girls were left to follow on behind. Alone in the Governor's House, the three grand duchesses busied themselves sewing copious quantities of jewels into their clothing—in their corsets, into belts and caps, and anywhere else they could be concealed. Should exile come, they were determined to be prepared.

Communications between Yakovlev and his revolutionary masters had already acquired an ominous note: The codename they used for the family was "The Baggage," while the Ipatiev House in Ekaterinburg, to which they were bound, was called the "House of Special Purpose."

Nicholas and Alexandra's arrival in the Urals was nightmarish. A large and hostile mob had gathered at the station threatening to lynch them; it took a face-off, with the troops setting up machine-gun posts, to get the crowd to disperse. On May 20, Olga, Tatiana, Anastasia, and Alexei arrived after an equally terrifying journey accompanied by hostile and lascivious soldiers, and the family was reunited.

Ipatiev House was very different from the Governor's House in Tobolsk. There was a high fence around it, which created a claustrophobic effect, and the prisoners were allowed only an hour's exercise a day (it was here, too, that the Romanovs were

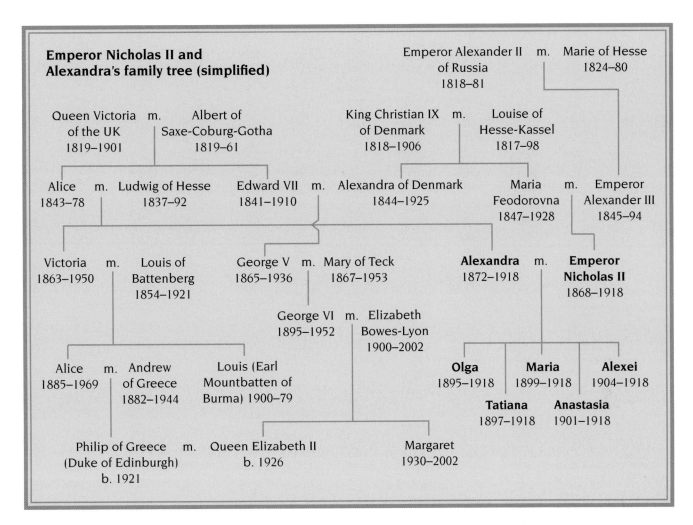

Emperor Nicholas II and Alexandra's family tree (simplified)

Emperor Alexander II of Russia 1818–81   m.   Marie of Hesse 1824–80

Queen Victoria of the UK 1819–1901   m.   Albert of Saxe-Coburg-Gotha 1819–61

King Christian IX of Denmark 1818–1906   m.   Louise of Hesse-Kassel 1817–98

Alice 1843–78   m.   Ludwig of Hesse 1837–92

Edward VII 1841–1910   m.   Alexandra of Denmark 1844–1925

Maria Feodorovna 1847–1928   m.   Emperor Alexander III 1845–94

Victoria 1863–1950   m.   Louis of Battenberg 1854–1921

George V 1865–1936   m.   Mary of Teck 1867–1953

Alexandra 1872–1918   m.   Emperor Nicholas II 1868–1918

George VI 1895–1952   m.   Elizabeth Bowes-Lyon 1900–2002

Alice 1885–1969   m.   Andrew of Greece 1882–1944

Louis (Earl Mountbatten of Burma) 1900–79

Olga 1895–1918   Maria 1899–1918   Alexei 1904–1918

Tatiana 1897–1918   Anastasia 1901–1918

Philip of Greece (Duke of Edinburgh) b. 1921   m.   Queen Elizabeth II b. 1926

Margaret 1930–2002

told that their routine was intended to resemble a prison regime). They were ordered to keep the windows shut—stifling in early summer's heat—and the panes were whitewashed so they could not look out. Most of the household had been forbidden to accompany them—even those who had traveled with them to Ekaterinburg, including the tutors Gilliard and Gibbes, were told when they reached the station that they could go no further.

FINAL DAYS

Yakov Yurovsky was appointed to take charge of "disappearing" the tsar and his family. Yakovlev and Lenin were careful; no communications were made that would allow any direct link between Lenin and the killings. Many would have been happy to see the tsar and the spectacularly unpopular Alexandra dead, but killing the four girls and Alexei, who was only 14 years old, would be unlikely to be widely accepted.

Yurovsky was a committed Bolshevik and a Tchekist—that is, a member of the state security organization. He later wrote a memoir, which came to be known as "the Yurovsky Note," which laid out in detail how he had planned the murders, and the many ways in which those plans had gone wrong. With a number of bodies to conceal, it was important that they be buried effectively. A week before the killings, Yurovsky and his henchmen researched a suitable spot, settling on a disused iron mine, called the Four Brothers, in woods a little way outside the town. A van was ordered to transport the bodies, and a cache of firearms laid in.

Family tree of Nicholas and Alexandra. *Largely thanks to the UK's Queen Victoria, "the Grandmama of Europe," in the early twentieth century a number of European rulers were closely related. Russia's Nicholas II and the UK's George V were first cousins through their mothers— sisters in the Danish royal family.*

The cellar in Ipatiev House. *The gunfire that killed the imperial family was so intense and protracted that it blew the plaster from the walls. This photograph was taken in 1919.*

THE MASSACRE IN THE CELLAR

On the evening of July 16, the family dined at around 8:30pm as usual, then had an early night, retiring at 10:30pm. Behind the scenes Yurovsky continued with his preparations. Accounts vary as to whether there were eight or ten killers—one or two backed out at the last minute, unwilling to kill Alexei and the girls. By 1:30am everything was ready. Each gunman had been assigned a target; the van was ready to take the bodies away.

Yurovsky roused Dr Botkin, told him that there was a disturbance in the town, and requested that he call the family together and ask them to ready themselves, as they were to be moved for their own safety.

The Romanovs were probably relieved: At last there would be a change in their grim routine. By 2am they had dressed and assembled downstairs, and Yurovsky led them across the courtyard and down into the cellar room on the opposite side. Nicholas was carrying Alexei, who still could not walk easily. Two chairs were brought for Alexandra and Alexei to sit down.

A minute later, the killers were led into the room. After a moment of confusion, Yurovsky read out the short statement he had prepared as a death sentence; there were gasps, and he remembered that the tsar only had time to exclaim "What? What?" before he shot him in the heart. His team followed suit, but were quickly blinded by smoke and deafened both by the shots themselves and by the revving of the van outside—which Yurovsky had ordered to cover the sound of shooting—and the scene degenerated into bloody chaos. Some of the killers had more enthusiasm for the task than others—when it became clear that the tsarevich and the grand duchesses were not all dead, Piotr

Some of the killers had more enthusiasm for the task than others ...

Ermakov, a career criminal before the Revolution and a devoted Tchekist since, began to stab them wildly with a bayonet. The diamonds sewn into Alexei's shirt and the girls' stays repelled the blade, and Ermakov's slashes became wilder and wilder until the cellar floor was slick with blood.

THE AFTERMATH

When it was finally over, the killers loaded the bodies onto the truck and drove out to the mine, where Ermakov had arranged to meet a team of extra men who would help bury them.

Yurovsky ordered that the bodies be stripped and their clothes burned. A further delay arose as the men discovered the concealed jewelry and began looting. Only the threat of being shot restored order among the men, and in the end the jewels were collected, and the bodies were burned and thrown down the mine. The situation turned to farce when it became clear that the "mineshaft" was only a few feet deep—no use for concealment at all.

By now it was morning. During the next two days, Yurovsky ordered a large quantity of petrol and an equal quantity of sulphuric acid, then returned to the forest and attempted to destroy the bodies. The first two brought out were those of Alexei and Maria, and he burned and buried them. It was slow work, however, and increasingly panic-stricken, he ordered a large pit to be dug a short distance away, put the remaining bodies inside, poured acid over them, and filled it in. The jewelry and precious items that had been left behind in the cellar and found on the bodies were gathered to be sent back to Moscow: they had a total weight of nearly 16 pounds (more than 7 kilograms).

The "burial" was finally completed at dawn on July 19. On the same day, the government gave a press release to the newspaper Pravda. It announced that the ex-tsar had been shot as White Russians threatened to take Ekaterinburg. It added that his wife and family had been sent "to a safe place."

DNA identification. DNA *was collected from family members of the Romanovs, both living and dead, to make a positive identification of the bones found in the forest near Ekaterinburg.*

Memorial shrine. *By the early 1990s, a modest wooden-roofed shrine in memory of the imperial family had appeared on the site of the now-demolished Ipatiev House.*

REDISCOVERY

The killings were not secret for long: Too many people knew about them. There was no immediate taste for recovering the bodies, however, and it was not until 1919, when the White Russian forces were once again in occupation of the Urals, that Nicholas Sokolov, a legal investigator, was charged by the local government to search for them. He was assisted by the imperial family's tutors, Gilliard and Gibbes, who were still living in Ekaterinburg, and he quickly discovered the Four Brothers mine, where a mass of fragments of clothing and small possessions were found—belt buckles, stays, buttons, and so on. There was also the gruesome find of a single body part: the severed finger of a middle-aged woman, "slender and manicured, like the empress's." Nothing else. Sokolov didn't believe that the killers could have destroyed the bodies so completely, but without full knowledge of the events of that horrific night's butchery, he didn't know where else to look.

... they started an experimental dig and quickly discovered skeletal remains, including three skulls.

Time passed, and the Soviets had full control of Russia. Over the decades it became taboo to discuss the Romanov assassination or to express curiosity about it. In the late 1970s, then-president Yuri Andropov ordered that Ipatiev House be bulldozed, lest it become a place of pilgrimage for mourners of the lost emperor. Shortly before his orders were obeyed a Moscow filmmaker, Geli Ryabov, visited the house and it piqued his interest. When he met a local amateur historian, Alexander Avdonin, the two decided to do a little digging. Avdonin had met Ermakov in his youth, and during their researches the pair uncovered a son of Yurovsky, who passed them a copy of the infamous Yurovsky Note, which he claimed—almost incredibly, given its contents—that his father had written as a lecture that had been delivered to his local Bolshevik group in 1934.

The text gave Avdonin and Ryabov plenty of pointers as to the location of the main grave. On May 30, 1979, they started an experimental dig and quickly discovered skeletal remains, including three skulls. They had found the Romanovs. Both knew, however, that it was not yet the time. After taking photographs of the bones, they laid them back in place and reburied them.

A decade later, Ryabov thought it would be safe to reveal their findings to the press. He gave a press interview in Moscow, telling all but taking the precaution of "moving" the site of the bodies about 500 yards/450 meters away from its real position. As it turned out, this was sensible, because a week after the interview was published, earthmovers arrived at the location he had given and removed tons of earth, taking it away completely. The true site, though, remained undisturbed. Finally, in 1991, Ryabov managed to interest Boris Yeltsin in his discovery. And this time, a team of professional archaeologists and pathologists digging at the correct site soon uncovered the bones—a tangled mass of partial skeletons. Their discovery was announced in the press on July 18, seventy-three years after the murders. However, only nine skulls were found, shattered into many pieces.

DNA was gathered from a number of sources, including the UK's Prince Philip (originally a prince of Greece, and a descendant of Queen Victoria), and the bones of Georgiy Romanov, Nicholas's younger brother who had died in 1899. The results were conclusive: The bones found were those of the last tsar, most of his family, and the doctor and servants who had been murdered with them. Although the patriarch of the Russian Orthodox Church refused to recognize the authenticity of the bones, they were given a formal burial in the crypt of the Peter and Paul Cathedral in St Petersburg on July 17, 1998, exactly eighty years after the Romanovs' execution.

But what of the separate burial site—the place where Tsarevich Alexei and the Grand Duchess Maria had been burned and buried? Fragments of bone that were identified—again through DNA tests—as belonging to them were uncovered in 2007, a little distance from the main grave site, exactly as Yurovsky had recorded. The Orthodox Church refused to recognize the authenticity of these bones, too, and at the time of writing, the last two members of the imperial family are still awaiting burial.

A large church, the sonorously named Church on Blood in Honor of All Saints Resplendent in the Russian Land, has been raised where the Ipatiev House once stood.

The grandiose Orthodox Church on Blood in Honor. *Inside the church, in Ekaterinburg, candles are kept perpetually alight in a shrine dedicated to Nicholas II as a martyred saint.*

MARTIN BORMANN

The date is October 1, 1946, and the Nuremberg Trials, held to bring Nazi war criminals to justice, are in full swing. Martin Bormann, Hitler's private secretary, has just been found guilty and sentenced to death. But he is not present to receive the verdict in person: He was tried in absentia, having vanished after Hitler's death. Now begins a worldwide search for him, fraught with false leads.

A T THE END of a reign of terror lasting more than a decade, in January 1945, the infamous Nazi leader Adolf Hitler took up residence in an underground bunker, located in the garden of the old Reich Chancellery in Berlin. Among those with him was Martin Bormann. When Hitler and his wife, Eva Braun, committed suicide on April 30, Bormann assisted with the cremation of the bodies—but then decided not to stick around to greet the Russian Red Army, who were approaching at speed.

KEEPING BAD COMPANY

Bormann and Hitler were of one mind when it came to politics. From his youth, Bormann was an advocate of pan-Germanism (the unification of all Europeans speaking German or a Germanic language), and although only in his late teens, he engaged in right-wing German Free Corps activities after World War I. In 1924, he was sentenced to a one-year prison sentence for acting as an accomplice in a political murder carried out by Rudolf Höss, the future commandant of the Auschwitz extermination camp, and after his release he joined Hitler's National Socialist German Workers' Party, commonly referred to as the Nazi Party.

Bormann's rise to a position of power was nothing short of meteoric—he became head of the Nazi press in 1926, and from 1928 was attached to the Supreme Command of the Sturmabteilung (SA), known as the Storm Troopers or Brownshirts, a paramilitary organization that adopted the violent intimidation of voters in local and national elections as a means to assist Hitler's rise to power. By 1930, he and the Führer were already chummy enough for Hitler to be named godfather to Bormann's first child, named Martin Adolf.

" ... a man's life and work go on after his death ... There is no such thing as death according to our view!" *–Martin Bormann*

Hitler's henchman. *Photographed in 1943, the year Bormann became secretary to the Führer and effectively took control of the Third Reich.*

Close associates. *Bormann chatting with Hitler outside the party headquarters in February 1943. The man on Hitler's left is Erwin Kraus, head of the National Socialist Motor Corps* (NSKK).

BORMANN THE BOOTLICKER

In 1933. Bormann was appointed chief of staff to Hitler's deputy, Rudolf Hess, replacing him in 1941 as head of the party chancellery. This gave him overall management of the Nazi Party's administration, including control over legislation, party appointments and promotions, and—after his appointment to the exalted post of Hitler's secretary in 1943—access of others to the Führer. "Bootlicker" was one of many unflattering words that was used to describe him at the time.

Like Hitler, Bormann was all for the persecution and extermination of Jews and Slavs, and for the German forced labor program. With that dark history, and an Allied victory threatening, it makes sense that he would have elected to escape from Germany with all possible speed when Hitler effectively surrendered by taking his own life. Bormann was last seen on May 2, 1945, crouching beside a German tank near Berlin's Weidendammer Bridge. He was heading for Lehrter railway station—and freedom.

Bormann meets 007

In 1996, a book was published making the bizarre claim that Winston Churchill (with the aid of *James Bond* author, Ian Fleming) had smuggled Bormann into England in order to help release Nazi gold held in Swiss bank accounts.

THE NUREMBERG TRIALS

When Bormann could not be found, it was assumed that he was either dead or in hiding, but because neither could be confirmed he was indicted on charges of war crimes on August 29, 1945, and tried in absentia. Twenty-four defendants were tried at Nuremberg in all, but one committed suicide while in prison, while another was deemed too unwell to be tried. After 216 court sessions before the International Military Tribunal, the verdict was handed down on the remaining twenty-two, who included Hermann Göring, Rudolf Hess, Joachim von Ribbentrop, and Wilhelm Keitel. Three defendants were acquitted; four received prison sentences ranging from ten to twenty years; three were sentenced to life imprisonment; the remaining twelve were sentenced to death. One—Göring—committed suicide ahead of the scheduled execution and ten were hanged on October 16, 1946. But Bormann, the twelfth condemned criminal, was still missing.

"Bormann is almost certainly dead, but his decease has not prevented numerous rumours as to his whereabouts gaining currency." —*Sir Percy Sillitoe, Director General of MI5*

THE WILD GOOSE CHASE

After Nuremberg, British agents searched for Bormann with an intensity bordering on mania, and his MI5 file records an array of spurious sightings around the globe. The description of the criminal they were seeking was very precise— "Bloated complexion, pale, almost Chinese yellow. Probably duelling scars on left cheek … a deep voice, bull neck and knock-kneed walk"—but it turned out that the world was teeming with Bormann lookalikes. He popped up in Germany,

The Nuremberg Trials. *Bormann was tried in absentia and sentenced to death, sparking a fruitless worldwide search in order to find and execute him. Front row, from left: Göring, Hess, von Ribbentrop, Keitel.*

sporting a traditional Tyrolean hat; in Tibet, sitting on a mountainside; in Switzerland, posing as an Israeli doctor; in Bolivia, Italy, Norway, Brazil, Sweden. On occasion, he was apparently accompanied by the Führer himself, looking—as one might expect—pale as a ghost. Bormann was even allegedly observed plotting a Nazi revival with the aid of a pile of world maps and a globe in a glass case. On this occasion, he was lurking by an airfield in Spanish Morocco … In total, more than six thousand sightings were reported.

BORMANN IN SOUTH AMERICA

Senior intelligence officials at MI5 were firmly convinced that Bormann was dead, and took all news of sightings with a pinch of salt—even when an "absolutely reliable German source" reported that he had disembarked from a submarine in the Argentine city of Posadas on July 29, 1945, and was now operating secret Nazi organizations from Chile. South America proved a popular continent for Bormann-spotting, and he was even arrested there, twice—in 1967, when the suspect turned out to be a Guatemalan peasant, and a few years later, when a completely innocent 72-year-old German was questioned in Colombia.

TWO SKELETONS IN BERLIN

In 1965, acting on the eyewitness account of Erich Kempka, Hitler's driver, the authorities in West Berlin dug up ground where, allegedly, the bodies of Bormann and of Hitler's personal surgeon, Ludwig Stumpfegger, were buried. The search revealed nothing, and resulted in jubilant neo-Nazis rekindling the myth that Bormann was alive—so in December 1972, another dig took place, this time on a derelict site near the Lehrter railway station. This time, two skeletons were discovered; splinters of glass cyanide capsules were found in the jawbones of the skulls, and it was concluded that Bormann and Stumpfegger had escaped from the bunker, become trapped by crossfire, and killed themselves with cyanide thoughtfully supplied by Hitler.

The search for remains. The first hunt for Bormann's remains, in Berlin's Invalidenstrasse, drew a blank. However, a second dig some years later, near Lehrter railway station, offered up a skeleton matching his description.

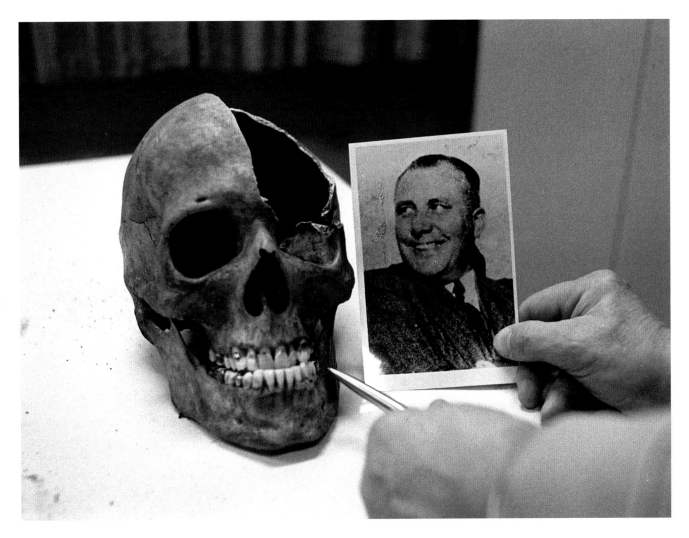

Early the following year, a forensic expert stated with "near certainty" that one of the skeletons was Bormann's, and he was declared officially dead on April 11, 1973. However, the authorities still erred on the side of caution and secured the remains in a cupboard at the Frankfurt Public Prosecutor's Office, refusing to release them to the family. So it wasn't quite over—and in 1993 a newspaper in the South American country of Paraguay reported that Bormann had spent the last three years of his life there, and died in Asunción in 1959. He was buried, the article asserted, in a nearby town.

THE DNA TEST

Eventually, in 1998, scientists compared DNA obtained from a piece of the skull thought to be Bormann's with a tissue sample obtained from an 83-year-old relative. The test revealed matching sequences, leading to this conclusion: "Based on this investigation, we support the hypothesis that the skeletal remains are those of Martin Bormann." So the matter is settled, and the body cremated in secret by German officials, its ashes scattered on the Baltic Sea in August 1999, was definitely Bormann's … or is there a touch of ambiguity in that wording that leaves us still wondering a little? Could it be that one of the world's wickedest men survived World War II—and the Nuremberg Trials—and really did live on, plotting doggedly, in South America?

EVA PERÓN

Eva Perón rose from obscurity to become a pivotal figure in Argentina's political history, even though her life was cut short within months of her thirty-third birthday. But if her life was extraordinary, her death was almost more so, because three years later her embalmed corpse was spirited away on a curious odyssey lasting almost two decades.

María Eva Duarte de Perón
Born: May 7, 1919, Los Toldos, Argentina
Spouse: Colonel Juan Perón (m. October 18, 1945)
Died: July 26, 1952, Buenos Aires, Argentina
Buried: Recoleta Cemetery, Buenos Aires, Argentina

MARÍA EVA DUARTE was born in Los Toldos, a small rural town in the pampas region of Buenos Aires Province, Argentina. She was the youngest of her mother's five illegitimate children; her father had a wife and another family, and Eva grew up no stranger to poverty. At the age of 15, she moved to the capital, Buenos Aires, to fulfill her ambition of becoming an actress—but her destiny lay elsewhere.

A MATCH MADE IN HEAVEN

Eva enjoyed considerable success as a stage and film actress, but it was on radio that she really found her métier. She started her own radio entertainment business, the Company of the Theater of the Air, and launched *Heroines of History*, a series about such illustrious women as Queen Elizabeth I of England, Catherine the Great of Russia, and the French actress Sarah Bernhardt—an inspiring ensemble indeed for Eva to emulate. But in 1945 Eva began to engage her oratorial skills for a completely different purpose—that of promoting her husband as candidate in the country's presidential elections.

Legend sets Eva's first encounter with Juan Perón against the worthy and romantic backdrop of a fundraiser held at the capital's Luna Park Stadium in 1944, in the wake of an earthquake that virtually destroyed the city of San Juan in western Argentina. Perón was born in 1895 in Lobos, Buenos Aires Province; he had entered military school at the age of 16, progressed through the officer ranks, and was promoted to colonel in 1941. In 1943, he took part in a military coup that overthrew Argentina's corrupt conservative government and used his position as secretary of labor and social welfare to enact social measures to support urban industrial workers. He was appointed vice president in 1944.

When Juan and Eva met, Perón was 48 years old and Eva just 24, but they had both come from a lowly background and understood financial hardship. Perón was charming and intelligent, and was tall and strong to Eva's petite build. They fell in love, fairy-tale style, and were married the following year. The happy couple were to become the voice of Argentina's working class, and when Perón was

Presidential glamor. *Juan and Eva Perón, painted by Numa Ayrinhac in 1948. To date, this is the only official portrait of an Argentine president to feature the First Lady.*

Last public appearance. *A frail Eva accompanies Juan on his second inaugural parade in June 1952, shortly before her death. She was reported to be supported by a "cage" concealed beneath her long fur coat.*

campaigning for the presidency, pledging himself a "man of the people," Eva was at his side—the first wife to accompany a candidate on a campaign tour. Perón was elected president in 1946 with the support of both workers and industrialists, and he and Eva gave birth to the only child they were to have: Peronism, the powerful political movement that lives on in Argentina even today.

EVA BECOMES EVITA

Perón gave Eva her own office and in her unofficial role at the Ministry of Health and Labor she became an advocate for the impoverished. In 1948, she launched the Eva Perón Foundation, replacing the existing Sociedad de Beneficencia, a charitable organization run by elderly upper-class women, and declaring that "when the rich think about the poor, they have poor ideas." With exceptional efficiency and drive, she organized the construction of schools, hospitals, and orphanages in underprivileged areas, as well as homes for single mothers and the elderly. When she visited Europe on a goodwill tour in 1947, she made sure to take every opportunity to learn about social policy in other countries in order to broaden her own knowledge to benefit Argentina.

To Argentina's poor laborers, the *descamisados* ("shirtless ones"), Eva was worthy of an earthly sainthood, and she became affectionately known to those who loved her as Evita, "little Eva." Not everyone revered her, however. There were those—possibly those who fell foul of her determination to take whatever measures necessary, including manipulation, to fund assistance for the poor— who described her as ruthless, a Nazi sympathizer, and an embezzler.

THE CENTURY OF VICTORIOUS FEMINISM

Eva was a leading light in Argentina's feminist movement, with the full support of Perón, who in 1944 had inaugurated the Women's Division of Work and Assistance. Asserting that the 1900s would go down in history as "the century of victorious feminism," Eva worked relentlessly for women's right to vote, to divorce and remarry, and to run for office, as well as for equal rights in the workplace and equal civil rights. The law granting women the right to vote was passed on

The Casa Rosado balcony

Shortly before Perón's election as president, the government sanctioned his arrest, his social policies proving a thorn in their side. He was detained for four days, until the workers of Buenos Aires gathered in the Plaza de Mayo outside the Casa Rosada, the presidential palace, and demanded the release of their leader. He famously reassured the crowd from the balcony of the palace on October 17, 1945. In the ensuing years, Eva too often addressed the *descamisados* from the balcony.

September 23, 1947, bringing the country into the modern age. On July 26, 1949, the newly formed Peronista Feminist Party, made up entirely of women, held its first national assembly and elected Eva as president. She opened the Salon Rosado in the congress building for the sole use of women politicians.

RENUNCAMIENTO

On August 2, 1951, the General Confederation of Labor (CGT), Argentina's largest Peronist trade union, asked Perón to run again for president, this time with Eva as vice president. The following day, at a huge rally, more than a million people expressed their support for Eva, and demanded to know if she would accept. She demurred, asking for time to consider, but the crowd insisted, "Now!" Eva appeared to relent and the crowd was satisfied; but within days, in a nationwide radio broadcast, she renounced her candidacy. At a rally on October 17, "Loyalty Day," she delivered an eloquent speech to the workers, thanking them for their support and hinting at her imminent death—the people's beloved Evita had been diagnosed with cervical cancer.

Eva exercised her right to vote in the elections for the first time—but it was also to be the last. She cast her vote from her sick bed and when she accompanied Perón to his second inauguration in June 1952, it was her last public appearance.

Nation's leader. *This image of Eva dominates the entrance to the Museo Evita in Buenos Aires, where the memorabilia on display includes her extravagant wardrobe.*

DEATH OF THE NATION'S SPIRITUAL LEADER

On July 26, 1952, the Subsecretariat of Information announced Eva's death: "It is our sad duty to inform the people of the Republic that Eva Perón, the Spiritual Leader of the Nation, died at 8:25pm." The news was met with a tremendous outpouring of grief by the workers, who were instructed to observe a period of thirty days' mourning, and all official activities ceased for two days. Perón ordered that all postage stamps be withdrawn and replaced with a memorial issue bearing his wife's portrait, and that the country's radio stations should not broadcast any lighthearted or humorous programs for the following thirty days. While the country's military and upper classes breathed a sigh of relief to be rid of Eva, the workers called for her canonization.

Loyalty Day, 1951. *The day that commemorates October 17, 1945, the foundation day of Peronism and the day in 1951 that Eva announced her intention not to run as vice president to Juan.*

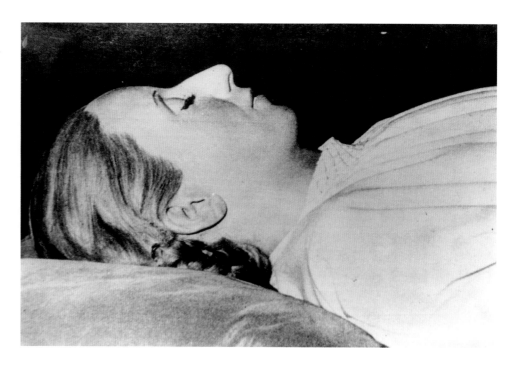

Rest in peace, Eva. Her emaciated body, ravaged by cancer, was hastily embalmed for the public viewing, followed by a full embalming that took several years to complete.

FOREVER BEAUTIFUL

Within hours of Eva's death, Dr Pedro Ara began the meticulous process of embalming the body in preparation for lying in state. An estimated two million people filed past Eva's glass-topped casket, draped with the Argentine flag, during the official thirteen-day mourning period, while an estimated three million witnessed her state funeral. Eva's corpse was then taken to a guarded room, her former office, in the CGT headquarters. Here Ara completed the lengthy and complicated embalming, which cost in the region of $100,000 (today, approaching $1 million); but Ara assured Perón that Eva's body would remain forever beautiful.

"I am Eva Peron, the wife of the President, whose work is simple and agreeable ... and I am also Evita, the wife of the leader of a people who have deposited in him all their faith, hope, and love." —*Eva Perón*

EVA TAKES A TRIP

Eva remained in the embalming room in the care of Dr Ara for three years, but after Perón was overthrown in a coup d'état in 1955, the new government, keen to erase any lingering threat of Peronism, secretly removed Eva's body with the intention of stashing it in an unmarked grave in Chacarita, the city's largest cemetery. Colonel Koening was tasked with the burial, but he was spooked when flowers and lighted candles appeared beside the parked truck containing the coffin, and failed to see it through. What happened next is a matter of speculation—Koening almost certainly hid the coffin in the attic of the military intelligence building, although a far more farcical (and hopefully untrue) version of events is that he secreted it in the apartment occupied by his deputy, who thought he heard an intruder breaking in to steal the body and fired a shot, only to discover that the "intruder" was his pregnant wife. Meanwhile, graffiti began to appear in the city: "Where is the body of Eva Perón?"

Determined to see Eva off once and for all, officials dispatched her to Italy, and this time they meant business—decoy coffins were sent out first to various Argentine embassies in Europe. Eva herself arrived on May 17, 1957, and was buried in a plain wooden coffin in Milan's Monumentale Cemetery under the false name of Maria Maggi. Here she stayed until 1971, when her remains were disinterred; the rotting wooden coffin was found to contain another, of silver with a glass top. Eva was transported to the home of Juan Perón, who was living in exile in Madrid, Spain, with his third wife, Isabel.

ISABEL PERÓN

Isabel painstakingly cleaned the body, even to the extent of washing and blow-drying Eva's dyed blonde hair. Eva's open casket is said to have been kept for a time— bizarrely—on the dining room table at Perón's villa. But her restless journey was not yet at an end. Perón returned to Argentina in 1973 and was once more elected president. He died the following year and Isabel succeeded him, becoming the world's first female president. She at once oversaw the repatriation of Eva's body, which was briefly put on display alongside Perón's. Isabel's plan to build a national monument to contain the two coffins never came to fruition, however—her presidency lasted less than two years, ending in March 1976.

A GRUESOME DISCOVERY

When it arrived in Madrid in 1957, Eva's corpse was found to be somewhat battered—there was a large dent in the nose, for example, and one fingertip was missing, believed to have been removed after the 1955 coup to verify Eva's identity. Back in Argentina her body was entrusted to Domingo Tellechea, an expert in restoration, to be made presentable for display. He observed that internally, at least, Eva was immaculately preserved, thanks to the skill of Dr Ara. But there was more to come. In 2011, Daniel Nijensohn, a neurosurgeon at Yale University Medical School, studied scans of X-rays taken of Eva's skeleton after death, and saw that her skull revealed signs of having been drilled. Nijensohn believes that, shortly before her death, Eva underwent a lobotomy to numb her emotional responses, possibly to help manage the pain of her illness, or perhaps to curb her increasingly erratic behavior. Either way, he is convinced that the operation hastened Eva's death.

EVERY DAY, FOREVER

In 1976, Eva was finally laid to rest in a fortified crypt deep underground, beneath her family's mausoleum in Recoleta Cemetery, Buenos Aires. On her death, the then secretary-general of the General Confederation of Labor, José Espejo, declared that a workers' delegation would place flowers on her tomb every day forever, and indeed flowers and notes appear at the entrance to the simple black tomb almost daily. And on July 26 every year, thousands gather there in memory of Eva, who had one of the most extraordinary lives—and deaths—in modern history.

A nation in mourning. *Tragically, Eva's own death led to several more, along with thousands of injuries suffered in the immense crush to view her body.*

CHE GUEVARA

Think of the quintessential modern revolutionary and the name that springs to mind is invariably that of Che Guevara, the Argentine-Cuban guerrilla leader whose handsome face gazes broodingly from an iconic image, recognized worldwide. Chilling photographs of Che laid out on a table confirmed his execution in 1967, but for thirty years the location of his body remained a closely guarded secret.

Ernesto Guevara de la Serna
Born: June 14, 1928, Rosário, Argentina
Spouse: 1. Hilda Gadea Acosta (m. 1955–59); 2. Aleida March (m. 1959–67)
Children: Hilda (1956–95), Aleida (b. 1960), Camilo (b. 1962), Celia (b. 1963), Ernesto (b. 1965)
Died: October 9, 1967, La Higuera, Bolivia
Buried: Santa Clara, Cuba

ERNESTO "CHE" GUEVARA DE LA SERNA, the eldest of five children, was born in Rosário, a city in Santa Fe province, Argentina, in 1928. His well-to-do parents both held radical political views and his literary diet comprised controversial leftist works, while his circle of friends included children of republican parents in exile after the Spanish Civil War of 1936–39. It was the perfect environment for the incubation of a revolutionary ideology.

THE MOTORCYCLE DIARIES

What's more, Rosário was a fitting birthplace for someone with Che's destiny—it was here that the first Argentine flag had been hoisted when the country gained independence from Spain in the wake of the so-called May Revolution of 1810. However, Che did not grow up there: He developed chronic asthma as a young child and his family moved to the mountains for the beneficial air. In 1947, he enrolled at the University of Buenos Aires, graduating with a degree in medicine in 1953; but before he completed his studies, he took a nine-month road trip through South America with a friend, which began as two young men on an adventure but was to shape the rest of his life.

Che set off in January 1952 with his traveling companion Alberto Granados, a biochemist who ran the dispensary at a leper center. Their means of transportation was a decrepit 1939 Norton 500 Model 18 motorcycle, dubbed La Poderosa, "Powerful." Their destination was North America. Sadly, the motorcycle met its end in Santiago, Chile, and was powerful no more. Che and Alberto took to hitchhiking instead; nonetheless, Che's record of the journey, published posthumously, is known as *The Motorcycle Diaries*.

At this point, various encounters began to have a profound impact on Che as he and Alberto witnessed poverty, exploitation, illness, and suffering. In Chile, they visited Chuquicamata, the world's largest open-pit copper mine; the primary source of the country's wealth, it was at that time run by US mining monopolies and

Destined for greatness. Che Guevara sporting his trademark beret and Cuban cigar. It was his view that "a smoke in times of rest is a great companion to the solitary soldier."

seen as a symbol of foreign domination. In Peru, they visited Hugo Pesce, a leprosy researcher and prominent Marxist, with whom Che enjoyed political discussions; he also discovered he had a rapport with the indigenous peoples. In the Amazon rainforest, they worked as volunteers at the San Pablo leper colony. By the time Che returned to Argentina, his social and political conscience was wide awake. His ambition was a unified, communist South America: "I will be on the side of the people," he wrote in his diary. "I will take to the barricades and the trenches, screaming as one possessed, will stain my weapons with blood, and, mad with rage, will cut the throat of any vanquished foe I encounter."

"I will be on the side of the people ..."—*Che Guevara*

CHE IN CUBA

The island of Cuba was settled by Spanish colonists soon after Columbus landed there in 1492, and remained a Spanish territory until finally liberated by the 1895–98 Cuban War of Independence. But by the 1950s, Cuba's welfare was in the hands of Fulgencio Batista, a brutal dictator. On July 26, 1953, a young lawyer named Fidel Castro launched an attack on Moncada Barracks, a federal garrison in Santiago de Cuba, in the first armed action of the revolution against Batista. The assault was a dismal failure. Many rebels were captured and executed, while Fidel was sentenced to fifteen years' imprisonment and his younger brother, Raúl, to thirteen years. However, in 1955 Batista released all political prisoners, including the Moncada rebels—a gesture he would soon regret.

CHE MEETS CASTRO

In 1954, Che met Ñico López, a survivor of the Moncada attack, in Guatemala. Che began to study Marxism, and when CIA-backed rebels arrived in Guatemala to overthrow the elected communist-leaning government in favor of military rule, he followed Jacobo Arbenz, the country's newly deposed president, to Mexico. Here, López arranged for Che to meet the Castro brothers, who had also fled to Mexico after their release from prison. It proved to be a true meeting of minds.

Che agreed to join the revolutionaries, and an invasion force landed in Cuba on December 2, 1956. The next two years saw the rebels engaged in guerrilla warfare, gaining increasing support as they headed toward Havana. On January 1, 1959, Batista fled the island and Castro became chief of state and head of government. Che was declared a Cuban citizen and appointed head of the

Che's letter to his children

Che wrote a letter to his five young children, to be read in the event of his death. It urged them to grow up as good revolutionaries; and "above all, always be capable of feeling deeply any injustice committed against anyone, anywhere in the world. This is the most beautiful quality in a revolutionary."

Che the family man.
Photographed here with his second wife, Aleida March, and their four children, Che also had a daughter with his first wife, Hilda Gadea.

In illustrious company. *Che Guevara shares a joke with Fidel Castro. It is said that, despite their very different personalities, the two men quickly became and remained deeply loyal friends.*

National Bank of Cuba and the department of industry of the National Institute of Agrarian Reform, and later became minister of industry—all roles for which he was unqualified and at which he failed spectacularly.

CHE THE BLOODTHIRSTY

Che's role in the revolution and its aftermath showed that he was more than prepared to kill for his cause—and, indeed, his detractors see him as nothing more than a ruthless murderer. As a soldier and comandante he ordered the execution of rebel deserters, and later earned himself the title of "the butcher of La Cabaña" (Castro's political prison) during the purge of Batista loyalists. He also oversaw the establishment of Cuba's forced labor camp on the Guanahacabibes Peninsula, the first of many concentration camps for the incarceration of the "unfit," from dissidents to homosexuals. Che made no secret of his bloodthirsty tendencies. In a 1967 message to the Tricontinental solidarity organization, he spoke of unbending hatred for the enemy making a human being into an "effective, violent, selective, and cold-blooded killing machine."

THE CUBAN MISSILE CRISIS

Castro aligned himself with the communist ideology of the Soviet Union, with whom the United States was engaged in the Cold War. Communism was by no means new to Cuba; the Cuban Communist Party was founded in 1925 and renamed the People's Socialist Party in 1944. In 1961, Castro merged the party with the 26th of July Movement, and Cuba became a Marxist-Leninist one-party republic. In August 1962, Che met Soviet leader Nikita Khrushchev to finalize details of a plan to make Cuba a nuclear beachhead. The United States broke off diplomatic relations with Cuba, imposing a trade embargo, the full lifting of which may be affected by the death of Castro and the election of Donald Trump as US president in 2016.

On October 14, 1962, an American spy plane passing over Cuba photographed a Soviet ballistic missile being assembled for installation. A week later, the US president, John Kennedy, advised the American people that he intended to enact a naval blockade around Cuba and, if necessary, use military force to neutralize the perceived threat to national security. Tension simmered

"Heroic guerrilla"
The mesmerizing black-and-white image that keeps Che in the public consciousness years after his death was taken at a political rally in Havana by the late Cuban photographer "Korda." Today it appears on a vast array of merchandise—Che the Revolutionary has become Che the Brand, completely at odds with everything he believed in.

Iconic image. *This 1960 image of Che is said to have been reproduced more often, and in more ways, than any other in the history of photography.*

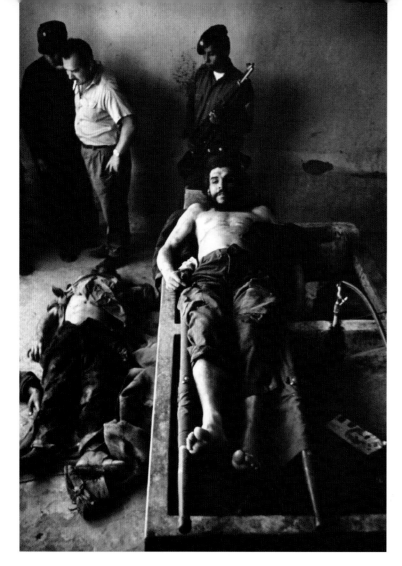

for a few days, almost bubbling over on October 24 when Soviet ships bound for Cuba approached US vessels enforcing the blockade, and again on October 27, when an American reconnaissance plane was shot down over Cuba and a US invasion force gathered in Florida. However, on October 26, with nuclear war imminent, Khrushchev offered to remove the missiles in exchange for the US promising not to invade Cuba. Two days later the crisis was over.

FAREWELL, FIDEL

In 1965, with the Cuban economy faltering as a result of the American trade sanctions and of Che's unsuccessful reforms, the zealous rebel decided his talents would be better directed toward fomenting revolution elsewhere in the developing world and he wrote to Castro to resign his leadership duties. His subsequent departure from the island spawned much speculation—had he died, or disappeared, and if so, where? Had he and Castro fallen out? To put all rumors to rest, Castro eventually read Che's letter to the Cubans, breaking his promise to Che to keep its contents a secret between them.

Death of an icon. Che's corpse on display to the world press in the laundry house of the Vallegrande hospital, Bolivia. Many commented on the similarity of his lifeless body to images of Christ crucified.

THE HISTORY OF A FAILURE

Meanwhile, on April 24, 1965, Che arrived in Africa in what is now the Democratic Republic of the Congo, leading a small expeditionary force of black Cuban fighters, descendants of African slaves imported by the early Spanish settlers. The Congo had gained independence from Belgium in 1960 and was suffering instability.

The US needed the Congo's natural resources—the republic is a rich source of cobalt, important in the weapons industry, and had supplied the uranium used in the atomic bomb dropped on Hiroshima in 1945. Che's mission was to "Cubanize" the Congolese so they could protect themselves from American imperialism. With Cuban reinforcements, he attempted to teach politics and military tactics to rebel forces, but soon concluded that they lacked revolutionary fervor. He wrote to Castro at length, explaining that "we can't liberate by ourselves a country that does not want to fight." Che and his men departed on November 21, 1965; three days later anticommunist Joseph Mobutu seized power to rule the Congo as a corrupt dictator, with US support. "This," wrote Che in his diary, "is the history of a failure."

CHE IS AMBUSHED

Undeterred by his experience in the Congo, Che moved on to the jungles of Bolivia to organize a guerilla war there. But it was not to be; Bolivia did not want a revolution. With CIA assistance, a manhunt was launched and Che was tracked down to his encampment. On October 8, 1967, Bolivian military forces ambushed him. The following day, he was photographed with his captors, bedraggled and defeated. He resisted interrogation, but blanched visibly when he was told there would be no trial. Soon afterward, he was executed.

Che's body was strapped to the landing shafts of a helicopter and transported to Vallegrande, where it was met by a huge military contingent and most of the town's inhabitants. Here, the body was cleaned up in a makeshift morgue and photographed for the press, who were informed that Che had died in a skirmish. His hands were severed from his corpse and placed in formaldehyde to preserve the fingertips for identification, should Castro claim the body was not Che's. And his executioners seized mementoes—Che's iconic pipe went to the soldier who shot him, his CIA interrogator took the tobacco, and an operative who snipped a lock of Che's hair auctioned it in 2007 for $100,000.

> "Do not shoot! I am Che Guevara and worth more to you alive than dead."
> —*Che Guevara, October 8, 1967*

GUEVARA MEMORIAL BUT NO CHE

December 28, 1988, saw the official opening of a memorial to Che Guevara in Santa Clara, Cuba. The site included a museum, a parade ground, and a 22-foot/7-meter bronze statue of Che with rifle in hand. All that was missing was a mausoleum containing Che's body—because his whereabouts were unknown. It was another nine years before a retired Bolivian general revealed that in the early hours of October 11, 1967, the bodies of Che and several other guerrillas had been thrown into a mass grave, dug hastily at the end of a dirt runway at Vallegrande airport. The general's memory of the exact location was a little hazy, so the operation to find and exhume the remains of Che and those buried with him took well over a year, and involved a forensic team and historians armed with mapping equipment.

On October 17, 1997, Che's remains were reburied beneath his memorial at Santa Clara with full military honors. With his ambition of a unified South America unfulfilled, he would no doubt be astonished to know that he has become such a symbol of hope for the poor of the world; but as Castro mused at his funeral, "Why did they think that by killing him, he would cease to exist as a fighter?"

Fitting memorial. *The Che Guevara Memorial in Santa Clara, Cuba, stands on the site of the decisive battle of the Cuban Revolution that resulted in the dictator, Fulgencio Batista, fleeing the island.*

IN MEMORY

Major A. Glenn Miller
0505273
U.S. Army Air Force- W. W. II
Born- Clarinda, Iowa-
March 1, 1904
Missing in Action-
Europe, Dec. 15, 1944
1943 - 1944
418th A.A.F.T.T.C.
ale University- Nev

I SUSTAIN TH

Sustineo

LOST FOR GOOD

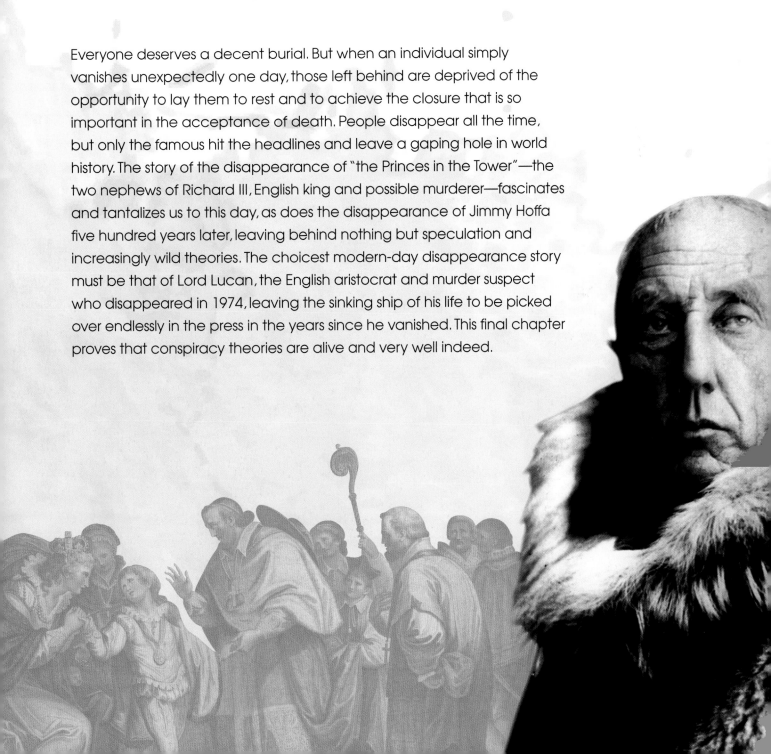

Everyone deserves a decent burial. But when an individual simply vanishes unexpectedly one day, those left behind are deprived of the opportunity to lay them to rest and to achieve the closure that is so important in the acceptance of death. People disappear all the time, but only the famous hit the headlines and leave a gaping hole in world history. The story of the disappearance of "the Princes in the Tower"—the two nephews of Richard III, English king and possible murderer—fascinates and tantalizes us to this day, as does the disappearance of Jimmy Hoffa five hundred years later, leaving behind nothing but speculation and increasingly wild theories. The choicest modern-day disappearance story must be that of Lord Lucan, the English aristocrat and murder suspect who disappeared in 1974, leaving the sinking ship of his life to be picked over endlessly in the press in the years since he vanished. This final chapter proves that conspiracy theories are alive and very well indeed.

THE PRINCES
IN THE TOWER

The year is 1483. Two young princes of the House of Plantagenet, Edward and Richard, lie fast asleep in their bed in the Tower of London. The door creaks open, and two men creep into the room. One holds a candle aloft, the other leans over and smothers the children with a pillow. Moments later, the princes are dead ... or are they?

Edward V
Born: November 2, 1470, London
Died: c.1483, London
Buried: 1678, Westminster Abbey, London (?)

Richard of Shrewsbury, Duke of York
Born: August 17, 1473, Shrewsbury
Died: c.1483, London
Buried: 1678, Westminster Abbey, London (?)

A CELEBRATED PAINTING MADE IN 1878 by the Pre-Raphaelite artist Sir John Millais depicts the 12-year-old King Edward V, yet to be crowned, clasping the hand of his younger brother, Richard. The boys, dressed from head to toe in black, are standing at the foot of the stairs to the Garden Tower, in the Tower of London, with fear and uncertainty in their eyes and gestures. They were right to be frightened—they were living in fearful times.

EDWARD V FAILS TO BE CROWNED

Edward, the son of Edward IV and Elizabeth Woodville, acceded to the throne on the death of his father on April 9, 1483. The royal House of Plantagenet was in the midst of a dynastic quarrel between its two branches, York and Lancaster— known as the Wars of the Roses— which after nearly thirty years was still rumbling on moodily, like a distant thunderstorm. Edward IV, of the House of York, had been on the throne throughout most of the conflict, interrupted only briefly in 1470 when the Lancastrian Henry VI—whom Edward had deposed in 1461—was reinstated, only to be imprisoned and murdered the following year.

Edward IV's reign was very successful. At first, he immersed himself in the export of wool and cloth, a major source of income in medieval times, in order to fill the Crown coffers, while his cousin Richard, Earl of Warwick, took care of the kingdom's government. Later, Edward became much more involved; in fact, so diligent and hardworking was he that he became exhausted, fell ill, and died at the age of 40.

There was one matter that proved contentious, however, and that was Edward's marriage to Elizabeth Woodville, the daughter of a nobleman but widow of a commoner. It led to a rift between Edward and Warwick (and ultimately to Warwick's demise in battle), but it was after Edward's death that it really became

Fear and uncertainty. *Sir John Everett Millais' emotive portrait of Edward and Richard,* The Princes in the Tower, *painted in 1878, nearly four hundred years after their disappearance.*

A fond farewell. *Prince Edward says farewell to his mother before traveling to London to claim the English throne following the death of his father, Edward IV.*

a problem. In his will, Edward appointed his brother Richard, Duke of Gloucester, as Protector should his successor, Edward V, be too young to rule—which, at the age of 12, he was. On May 4, the young king arrived in London with his brother, and arrangements were made for his coronation on June 22; but before that date was reached, the Bishop of Bath and Wells informed the Protector that when Edward married Elizabeth Woodville, he was already betrothed to Lady Eleanor Talbot—which, in those days, was as good as being married to her. This meant that the marriage to Elizabeth Woodville was invalid—and Edward and Richard were illegitimate.

Edward V now became the first of only two English kings to accede to the throne but not to be crowned—the other is Edward VIII, who famously abdicated in 1936 in order to marry the American divorcée Wallis Simpson. When Parliament met three days after the startling revelation about young Edward's ineligibility to the throne, the only option that presented itself was to approve a proposal that his Protector, Richard of Gloucester, should be crowned Richard III. Richard's coronation took place on July 6, in a ceremony of unprecedented magnificence, but just over two years later he was killed at the Battle of Bosworth, bringing an end to the Wars of the Roses—and the squabbling House of Plantagenet—and heralding a powerful new dynasty that finally united the two factions, the Tudors.

Malmsey wine

George, Duke of Clarence, brother of Edward IV and Richard III, was executed for treason in 1478, reputedly being drowned in a butt of malmsey, a strong, sweet white wine. This no doubt gave rise to the rumor that his nephews, the princes, met the same fate.

THE DOLOROUS END OF THOSE BABES

But back to the summer of 1483, and the deposed King Edward V and his unfortunate brother—who was also removed from the Yorkist bloodline—were lodged in the Tower of London. At that time it served as a royal residence, but also a prison … Robert Fabyan reported in *The Great Chronicle of London* (*c*.1512) that the two boys were seen "shooting [at butts of straw] and playing in the gardens of the Tower by sundry times"—enjoying the last of the summer sunshine, and perhaps also their last days. Gradually they were seen less and less, only occasionally appearing at barred windows in the Garden Tower where they lived with one servant, the (probably) prophetically named William Slaughter. And then they were no longer seen at all. Sir Thomas More, in *The History of King Richard* III, described their disappearance as "the dolorous end of those babes."

THE RUMORS START TO FLY

By the spring of 1484, according to Fabyan, there was "much whispering among the people" that the princes were dead, and soon it was rumored that they were not merely dead, but had been murdered. Smothered in their bed, poisoned, drowned in malmsey wine … suggestions as to the method came thick and fast. Then in March 1485, Richard III's wife, Anne Neville, died and it was rumored that he had poisoned her so he could marry the princes' oldest sister, Elizabeth

of York. He protested, of course, that "it never came into his thought or mind to marry in such manner," and whether that was true or not we shall never know. But mud sticks—and if Richard had poisoned his wife, had he also killed his two young nephews for the crown? Within a few years, his reputation as murderer of the Princes in the Tower was forged; but he was not the only candidate.

Death of innocence. A *macabre depiction by the nineteenth-century English painter James Northcote of the two young princes about to meet their "dolorous end" as they sleep in the Tower of London.*

INNOCENT SOULS

Around 1513, Sir Thomas More cleared up the mystery in his *History of King Richard* III—at least, he put forward his version of events, biased heavily against Richard. According to More, Richard charged his loyal servant Sir James Tyrell with making arrangements to "put the two children to death." The deed was carried out by two men, Miles Forest and John Dighton, who smothered them with their bedclothes until "their breath failing, they gave up to God their innocent souls." Tyrell is said to have confessed to his part in the murder shortly before he was executed for treason in 1502.

The princes, meanwhile, had been secretly interred in "such a place as … could never come to light." In fact, they did come to light, more than two hundred years later, or so it was assumed. In 1674, workmen demolishing a stone staircase leading to the Chapel of St John in the White Tower discovered an elm chest buried 10 feet/3 meters below ground and containing the skeletons of two children. Charles II's chief surgeon having assessed the remains to be "proportional to ages of those two brothers," it was concluded that these were indeed the princes, and four years later, on the orders of Charles, the bones were reinterred in the Innocents' Corner in Westminster Abbey.

DID HENRY STAFFORD DO IT?

Another possible culprit was the Lancastrian Henry Stafford, Second Duke of Buckingham, who had a claim to the throne based on the fact that he was the great-grandson of John of Gaunt, the third son of Edward III (to add to the confusion, Stafford also became the third husband of Margaret Beaufort, Henry VII's mother, another great-grandchild of John of Gaunt). Stafford was instrumental in putting Richard III on the throne but immediately began plotting to overthrow him. He had publicly denied the legitimacy of Edward V—had he also murdered him, along with his brother?

> "These brothers ... were privately and meanly buried, by the order of their perfidious uncle Richard the Usurper."
>
> —*Inscription on the princes' monument, Westminster Abbey*

OR WAS IT HENRY TUDOR?

Henry Tudor was the legitimate Lancastrian heir and claimant to the throne. Suspicion falls on him because, having defeated Richard III in battle and taken the crown, he was certainly not above bumping off anyone else who posed a threat to him, including the rival claimants Edward Plantagenet, son of Edward IV's brother George, and Perkin Warbeck, a young Flemish merchant who appeared in 1491 claiming to be Richard, the younger of the two vanished princes. But in 1486 Henry had married the princes' sister, Elizabeth of York, and repealed the *Titulus Regius*, the statute that declared the illegitimacy of Edward IV's children—including, of course, Elizabeth and the two princes. Thus they were all legitimized, and Henry acknowledged Edward V as his predecessor—but was this all just a smoke screen to cover up the fact that he had murdered the princes?

PERKIN WARBECK, PRETENDER TO THE THRONE

In 1768, Horace Walpole, whose father Robert was Great Britain's first prime minister, published *Historic Doubts on the Life and Reign of King Richard the Third*, in which he acquitted the much maligned king of the princes' murder. There are events that certainly point to his innocence—for example, if Perkin Warbeck was not a "pretender" at all but was in fact the younger prince, as some now believe, then he

A short reign. Edward held the title "King Edward V" for only a few weeks between his father's death and his own mysterious disappearance. He was never crowned.

Elizabeth Woodville, the White Queen

After their disappearance, the princes' mother, Elizabeth Woodville, remained on good terms with her brother-in-law, Richard III—surely a clue that she did not hold him responsible for her sons' disappearance. However, it has also been suggested that Elizabeth conspired with Henry Tudor—the future king and her future son-in-law—to spirit the princes safely away from the Tower of London.

was still very much alive several years after Richard III's death. Henry VII's reaction to Warbeck's claim is very significant—would he really have ordered the execution of the two high-profile figures behind the plot—the Dean of St Paul's Cathedral and the Lord Chamberlain—if he had nothing to fear? And if Warbeck had no valid claim, would he have persisted in his endeavor, to the extent of garnering the support of Maximilian, the Holy Roman Emperor?

The fact that Warbeck came from Flanders adds credence to a post-Tudor theory that, far from murdering the princes, Richard dispatched them to continental Europe to keep them safe from Lancastrian plotting. This left him in the awkward position of being rumored to have murdered the boys while being unable to produce them as proof of his innocence without putting them in the very danger from which he was attempting to shield them, so they remained on mainland Europe, undiscovered. Warbeck's own version, however, was that Edward had in fact been murdered by one of the men appointed to do the deed, while the other man had lost his nerve and helped Richard to escape.

THE SECRETS OF A PAINTING

The murder of innocent children is the most emotive of all crimes, and a far happier version of events is the theory that the princes were not killed at all but grew up under assumed names. In the 1990s, an amateur historian, Jack Leslau, drew attention to a portrait of Sir Thomas More and his household, painted aorund 1530 by the Tudor court artist Hans Holbein the Younger. According to Leslau, the painting is rich in symbolism that proves the princes remained alive and well. Leslau went further, asserting that Edward, renamed Sir Edward Guildford, was passed off as the eldest son of the Comptroller to the Royal Household, while Richard became Dr John Clement, President of the Royal College of Physicians (and, incidentally, married Sir Thomas More's daughter). A staunch Catholic, he fled England at the Reformation and lived to a ripe old age.

Mortal remains. *This marble monumental urn, designed by Sir Christopher Wren and set into the wall of Westminster Abbey's Lady Chapel, contains what are assumed to be the bones of the two young princes.*

DO NOT DISTURB

Attempts to get to the truth—or at least nearer to it—through DNA testing have so far been thwarted. Leslau unfortunately died before implementing his plan to compare the DNA of Sir Edward Guildford, who was buried in Chelsea Old Church in London, with that of Dr Clement, buried in Mecklen, Belgium. And the Church of England has consistently refused requests to exhume the remains of the two children in Innocents' Corner for forensic testing. In 1995, the then Dean of Westminster Abbey took advice from an historian and an archaeology professor, and the conclusion was that no amount of testing could reveal "the truth of the affair." Today, the Abbey's position is still that "the mortal remains of two young children, widely believed since the seventeenth century to be the princes in the tower, should not be disturbed."

LOUIS LE PRINCE

There is nothing more exciting than a new invention, and nothing more dangerous than several inventors having the same idea at the same time. In 1890, Louis Le Prince was on the verge of presenting to the world the first ever moving film—and then he vanished. Did he commit suicide, or is there a far more sinister explanation?

Louis Aimé Augustin Le Prince
Born: August 28, 1841, Metz, France
Spouse: Elizabeth Whitley (m. 1869)
Children: Marie (b. 1871), Adolphe (b. 1872)
Died: c. September 16, 1890, Dijon, France
Buried: unknown

CINEMATOGRAPHY IS ONE of the most significant innovations of all time, so it is not surprising that several countries clamor to claim its invention as their own. The United States waves the flag for the resourceful Thomas Edison, while France responds with the pioneering Lumière brothers. But for many the real but forgotten father of cinematography is Frenchman Louis Le Prince, who spent much of his life in the UK and US.

A CREATIVE AWAKENING

Louis Le Prince grew up learning about photographic processes from Louis Daguerre, a family friend and inventor of the daguerreotype. He studied chemistry and physics at university, and in 1866 joined an engineering company in Leeds, England, at the invitation of a fellow student, John Whitley. A town in England's industrial north might seem an odd environment for a creative awakening, but Leeds was in fact a flourishing center for the arts, and Le Prince became interested in the firing and painting of pottery, and then in photography. Le Prince married Whitley's sister, Lizzie, an artist, in 1869, and together they set up the Leeds School of Applied Arts.

In 1882, Le Prince moved his family to New York. Here, a visit to a panorama exhibition, where glass lantern slides were projected to simulate continuous movement, inspired him with a new possibility—creating moving pictures through photography. He patented his first invention, a sixteen-lens camera and projection system, in both the United States and England as a method "For Producing Animated Pictures of Natural Scenery and Life." However, it produced only a rather jerky approximation of a moving film and, back in Leeds, Le Prince set to work on a single-lens camera.

Pioneer of cinematography. *Louis Le Prince* (opposite), *photographed in 1870. His first attempt at a moving picture camera* (above) *had 16 lenses producing sequential photographs that simulated movement.*

A fleeting moment on film.
Traffic Crossing Leeds
Bridge, *shot one October day
in Victorian England, 1888.
It was captured by Le Prince in
20 frames on Eastman's paper-
strip photographic film.*

THE FIRST MOVING PICTURE

On October 14, 1888, Le Prince used his camera to film the first ever moving picture. *The Roundhay Garden Scene* depicts his son Adolphe marching determinedly in a circle, as directed by Le Prince, while his bemused in-laws and a friend rotate on the spot. Next came *Traffic Crossing Leeds Bridge*, preserving for posterity two seconds of life on a bustling street in late Victorian England. This film was the first to be projected on to a screen, achieved by slotting gelatin positives mounted on glass into a continuous belt, passed in front of a powerful arc light.

The crucial next step was to replace the glass with something stronger, lighter, and heat resistant, and this is where the magic of cinematography really began—with transparent celluloid roll film. It was now time for Le Prince to demonstrate his invention in the United States, and Lizzie and Adolphe selected the Jumel Mansion, Manhattan's oldest house, as the venue. The scene was set—but Le Prince was a no-show.

LE PRINCE VANISHES

Le Prince visited his brother in Dijon, France, before setting off for the United States. On September 16, 1890, he boarded a train bound for Paris, where he was to meet friends; from here, he planned to return to Leeds to collect his equipment and then to set sail for the United States from Liverpool. But Le Prince did not arrive in Paris. The train was searched from end to end, as was the railway track between Dijon and Paris, but there was no body, nor any sign of Le Prince's luggage. He had vanished into thin air and was never seen again.

WILD SPECULATION

Theories about Le Prince's fate were rife. Suicide was a popular notion—Le Prince, it was speculated, had been struggling financially. Yet there was no evidence to support this, and in any case he had been in Dijon to collect his share of an inheritance. But that fact led to another notion, that his brother had killed him after a row over their mother's will. It was even suggested that Le Prince's family had discovered him to be gay, and asked him to quietly lose himself. Lizzie

Adolphe Le Prince
Adolphe features in the last of Le Prince's film experiments, animatedly playing his accordion on the steps of his grandfather's house. Tragically, in 1901 this cheerful young man was found dead with his duck-hunting gun at his side. His mother was convinced that he, too, had been murdered.

and Adolphe, however, firmly believed he had been murdered by rivals—and the most likely candidate was American inventor Thomas Edison.

THE EDISON COURT CASE

After Le Prince's death, several versions of a moving picture camera were produced, and inevitably the issue arose of royalty payments for use of the process. Among the inventors was Edison, who in 1898 brought a case against American Mutoscope, a motion picture company founded in 1895, for patent infringement. Adolophe appeared as a witness for the defense, but was not permitted to show his father's two cameras as evidence, and the court ruled in favor of Edison as the first and sole inventor of cinematography. However, in 1902 the US Court of Appeals overturned the decision on the grounds that Edison did not own rights to the entire concept of the movie camera—but it made no difference to Le Prince, who was officially declared dead in 1897.

MYSTERY SOLVED?

Two clues as to Le Prince's fate have recently come to light. The first is a photograph, unearthed in 2003 in the Paris police archives, of a drowned man resembling Le Prince; the photograph was taken in 1890. The second is even more chilling. In 2008, a student of photography at the University of New York discovered a dilapidated journal with some of Thomas Edison's papers in the New York Public Library. An entry dated September 20, 1890, reads: "Eric called me today from Dijon. It has been done. Prince is no more. This is good news but I flinched when he told me. Murder is not my thing. I'm an inventor and my inventions for moving images can now move forward." An expert subsequently confirmed that the handwriting was Edison's ...

Commemoration at last. Although this blue plaque on Leeds Bridge in northern England concedes that Le Prince's frames were only "probably" the world's first successful moving pictures.

"It has been done. Prince is no more." —*Thomas Edison*

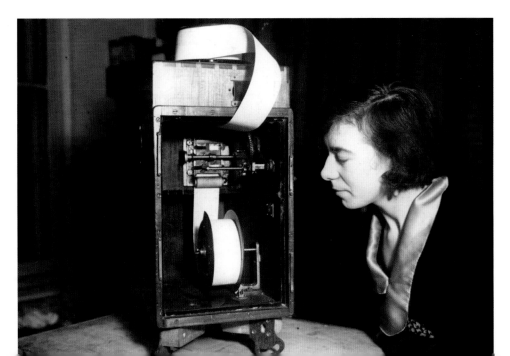

Le Prince's single lens camera. His daughter, Marie, donated the camera to the Science Museum in London; it is now on display in the National Media Museum in Bradford, England.

ROALD AMUNDSEN

The Norwegian explorer Roald Amundsen was the first to sail the Northwest Passage, the first to trek to the South Pole, and the first to fly across the Arctic. He was a sailor at heart, and fittingly he is buried in the depths of the ocean, although it was due to a plane crash in an unknown location, possibly somewhere in the Barents Sea.

Roald Engelbregt Gravning Amundsen
Born: July 16, 1872, Borge, Norway
Died: June 18, 1928, Arctic Ocean
Buried: At sea

THE SEA WAS IN AMUNDSEN'S BLOOD—he was born into a wealthy seafaring family, and although he started studying medicine, it was his mother's ambition for him rather than his own. When she died, Amundsen abandoned his studies and took to the waves. His inspiration was the British Arctic explorer Sir John Franklin, who died attempting to locate the elusive Northwest Passage.

NEGOTIATING THE NORTHWEST PASSAGE

The quest to find a route linking the Atlantic and Pacific oceans via the treacherous Arctic Archipelago had been challenging explorers since 1497, when the navigator John Cabot made the first endeavor. Many other famous explorers subsequently tried, failed, even died in the attempt, and in 1845 it was Franklin's turn to try. He and his crew also died—but their story fired Amundsen's imagination and from childhood it was his ambition to achieve what no one else had.

Between 1897 and 1899, Amundsen gained experience of surviving in extreme conditions on a scientific expedition to the Antarctic, when his ship became stuck in pack ice. This prepared him for when he and his six-man crew set sail in 1903 in search of the Northwest Passage in *Gjøa*, a converted 47-ton herring boat. It took three years to complete the journey; in 1905 they emerged into the Beaufort Sea, having negotiated the complex section of the passage that had defeated all earlier hopefuls, and the following year arrived in Nome, Alaska, on the Bering Sea, the northernmost part of the Pacific. "My boyhood dream," wrote Amundsen in his diary, "at that moment it was accomplished."

RACE TO THE SOUTH POLE

Amundsen's next goal was to reach the North Pole—but when he heard that an American explorer, Robert Peary, had already claimed it, he immediately decided to "turn to the right-about, and face to the South." He kept his plans a secret, however; he did not wish to be thwarted a second time, especially as the British explorer Captain Scott was also preparing his Antarctic expedition.

Intrepid explorer. *Roald Amundsen, clad in furs to combat the harsh Antarctic conditions. Familiarity with Nordic winters gave him the edge when planning his expeditions.*

In his anxiety to reach the South Pole before Scott, Amundsen almost ruined his chances at the outset by setting out from his base in severe weather, and he was forced to retreat or perish. He wisely decided on retreat, concluding that to risk the lives of men and sled-dogs was counter-productive. The expedition set off again a few weeks later, and completed the 800-mile/1,300-kiolmeter-plus journey on skis to plant the flag on the South Pole on December 14, 1911. Scott's party arrived more than a month later and sadly perished on the return leg.

NORTH POLE EXPEDITIONS

Amundsen's vessel on his triumphant Antarctic expedition to the South Pole was the *Fram*, on loan from his fellow countryman and explorer Fridtjof Nansen. In 1918, Amundsen embarked on an expedition in a new ship, the *Maud*, his aim to reach the North Pole by drifting across the Arctic Ocean, carried by the ice, or at least to get nearer than Nansen had in an earlier experiment in the *Fram*. Amundsen made two attempts, the second starting in 1922, but both failed.

AMUNDSEN TAKES TO THE AIR

Amundsen then joined the new breed of aviation pioneers, and in 1925 he and the American explorer Lincoln Ellsworth attempted to fly to the North Pole in two Dornier seaplanes. They got within 120 miles/190 kilometers of the pole. The following year, they tried again in a much lighter craft, the Italian airship *Norge*, and this time were successful, becoming the first to cross the Arctic by air. The pilot was the airship's designer, Umberto Nobile.

After the *Norge* flight, Amundsen and Nobile argued over who should receive credit for leading the expedition, and in 1928 Nobile set out as sole leader of another expedition. He successfully crossed over the North Pole but his craft, the *Italia*, crashed onto pack ice on the return journey. A huge rescue operation was mounted—and among those searching for Nobile was his rival, Amundsen.

Historic flight. *The airship* Norge *sets off from Kings Bay, Svalbard, Norway, in 1926, carrying a party of sixteen, including Amundsen, and a dog named Titina.*

The Antarctic conquered. Amundsen's Antarctic expedition success (left and below) was rewarded with personal telegrams of congratulations from the US president, Theodore Roosevelt, and Britain's King George V.

NOBILE IS FOUND—BUT AMUNDSEN IS LOST

On June 21, 1928, it was reported that Nobile had been sighted and an Italian seaplane had dropped supplies via parachutes near his camp. It was impossible to land the plane on the ice, but Nobile and his team now had the means to survive until they could be rescued.

Nobile was safe, but concern was now growing about Amundsen. His plane, a Latham 47 twin-engined flying boat, had taken off at 4pm on June 18 and a distress call was received at 6:45. Since then, there had been no further communication. Had the pilot made a forced landing on the ice somewhere, and were the would-be rescuers now in need of rescue themselves? A search was launched; on August 31, a torn-off wing float was found off the coast of Tromsø on the Barents Sea, and in October a gasoline tank was found at Haltenbanken in the Norwegian Sea, but by then all hope was lost and the Norwegian government had called off the search. Amundsen and his five crew members had vanished.

LOST FOR ETERNITY

In 2003, a retired Norwegian seal-hunter recalled how, in 1964, he had repaired a hut using a piece of driftwood that he now realized could have been plywood from Amundsen's plane. The memory was perhaps triggered by the discovery that year of a navigational chart on which was marked the position where a large object, possibly from the Latham's wing, had been snared by a fishing boat in 1933. The object had slipped away before the boat captain could land it, but if it was indeed from Amundsen's plane, it pinpointed the crash to somewhere near Bjørnøya (Bear Island) in the Svalbard archipelago in the Barents Sea. The following year, the Norwegian Aviation Museum attempted to locate the wreckage of the plane, but bad weather halted the mission.

In 2009, the Royal Norwegian Navy carried out an extensive search operation. Taking part were *Tyr*, a naval minesweeper, and *Harstad*, a coast guard vessel equipped with sonar, but the key apparatus was a bright orange, fully automated search robot, the HUGIN 1000, capable of making high-resolution maps of the seabed. The robot was programmed to focus on a 45-square-mile/117-square-kilometer area, where the wreckage of Amundsen's plane was thought to lie about 1,300 feet/400 meters deep.

No trace was found, however, and there are no plans for further investigations. Unless there is a change of heart, Amundsen—Norway's national hero and one of the world's greatest explorers—is lost for eternity.

> " The mystery will probably remain forever, because Amundsen could be anywhere within the Barents Sea." —*Rob McCallum, expedition leader, 2009*

AMELIA EARHART

Amelia Earhart was many things—feminist, fashion icon, trailblazer—but most of all she was America's "queen of the air." In 1932, this seemingly fearless young woman became the first aviatrix to fly solo and nonstop across the Atlantic Ocean; but five years later she vanished, apparently without trace, while trying to circumnavigate the globe. But did she, in fact, leave traces?

AMELIA EARHART WAS BORN on July 24, 1897, in Atchison, Kansas, and spent much of her childhood at the home of her maternal grandparents. She was a tomboy, enjoying the outdoor life, and became an independent young woman, firmly believing that women should assert themselves to find their place in the world. In 1920, Amelia took an airplane ride at the Winter Air Show in Long Beach, California—and her destiny was settled.

LADY LINDY IS BORN

Amelia immediately set to work to earn enough money to pay for flying lessons. Her first instructor was the pioneer aviatrix Anita "Neta" Snook, her second John "Monty" Montijo, who taught her how to fly solo and perform aerobatics. She gained her Fédération Aéronautique Internationale pilot's license (No. 6017), issued May 16, 1923, only the sixteenth woman to do so, and joined the Long Beach Air Circus, displaying her skills in shows on the airfield (now Long Beach Airport) belonging to renowned aviator Earl S. Daugherty.

Financial constraints kept Amelia from the world of aviation for a few years, but in 1927 she joined the American Aeronautical Society's Boston chapter; she also invested in Massachusetts' Dennison Airport, became a sales representative for Kinner airplanes, and penned a few articles promoting flying. Then in 1928 she received a phone call from pilot and publicist Captain Hilton H. Railey, inviting her to become the first woman to fly the Atlantic Ocean. Amelia's initial excitement soon gave way to disappointment when she discovered that she was to make the crossing not as the pilot, but as a passenger. However, the flight, in a Fokker F7 called *Friendship*, catapulted her into the eye of the public, and more importantly grabbed the attention of George Putnam, a publisher, who saw the

Pilot and style icon. *Amelia, smiling widely, sports her signature flying jacket (opposite). In formal photographs (below), she was careful to conceal the gap in her teeth.*

potential for a bestseller: 20 Hrs. 40 Min., named for the time taken to complete the flight. Amelia became a celebrity, America's "sweetheart" of the day.

But she was first and foremost an aviatrix, and because she was tall with a slender, boyish figure and bore a marked resemblance to Charles Lindbergh, "Lucky Lindy," who in 1927 had made the first solo nonstop flight across the Atlantic in the Spirit of St. Louis, she became known as "Lady Lindy." She campaigned for commercial air travel and promoted the newly incorporated Transcontinental Air Transport company. She competed in the first Santa Monica to Cleveland Women's Air Derby in 1929, was elected an official for the National Aeronautic Association, and in 1931 set the women's autogiro altitude record at 18,415 feet/5,613 meters. But in the back of her mind was the memory of that transatlantic flight as a passenger, and a comment she made afterward: "Maybe someday I'll try it alone."

Amelia's favorite planes

The Canary Amelia purchased her first aircraft in July 1921—a bright yellow Kinner Airster biplane, which she named "The Canary." The following year, she broke the women's altitude record in the plane, rising to a height of 14,000 feet/4,267 meters.

Old Bessie, the fire horse In 1930, Amelia bought a bright red Lockheed Vega 5B monoplane. She flew her "little red bus" on both her solo transatlantic flight and her nonstop coast-to-coast flight in 1932. Old Bessie is now on display at the Smithsonian National Air and Space Museum in Washington, DC.

The Flying Laboratory In 1936, the Purdue Research Foundation funded the purchase of Amelia's new twin-engined Lockheed 10-E Electra, the airplane she would fly on her ill-fated global circumnavigation attempt. Its intended use was as a test bed for new equipment—hence the nickname.

Old Bessie. *The six-seater bright red Lockheed Vega was a favorite of early aeronautical record setters. A number of modifications were made to Old Bessie before Amelia flew the plane solo across the Atlantic in 1932.*

Record breaker. *Amelia in the Hammond Model Y prototype entered in the Bureau of Air Commerce "safe airplane" competition in 1934.*

THWARTED BUT UNDEFEATED

In 1931, Amelia and George Putnam were married and immediately set about planning the coveted solo flight. On May 20, 1932, the fifth anniversary of Lindbergh's celebrated crossing, Amelia took off from Harbour Grace, Newfoundland. Her destination was Paris; however, adverse weather conditions conspired with mechanical malfunction to prevent her reaching that goal, and after a 2,026-mile/3,261-kilometer flight lasting just under fifteen hours she landed instead in pastureland near Derry in Northern Ireland, startling the Gallagher family who owned the farm and "scaring most of the cows in the neighborhood."

A GLORIOUS STRING OF "FIRSTS"

Safely back on American soil, Amelia became the first woman to be awarded a National Geographic Society Gold Medal and a Distinguished Flying Cross, presented by President Herbert Hoover and Congress respectively. She recorded her exploits in another book, *The Fun Of It.*

Amelia was now in her record-breaking element, and just two months later, on August 24–25, 1932, she set the women's nonstop transcontinental speed record, flying the 2,447.8 miles/3,3939.4 kilometers from coast to coast of the United States in nineteen hours and five minutes—a record she broke herself

> "The woman who can create her own job is the woman who will win fame and fortune." —*Amelia Earhart*

The Ninety-Nines

In 1929, Amelia helped organize "The Ninety-Nines" (named for its ninety-nine charter members), an international organization for female pilots, becoming its first president in 1931. The organization, still flourishing today for "women who love to fly," purchased Amelia's childhood home in 1984 and opened a museum in her memory.

under a year later. Also in 1932 she gained the first Gimbel National Award for an "outstanding American woman." In 1935, she racked up three more "firsts," including becoming the first person to fly solo from Hawaii to California, and thus the first to fly solo across both the Atlantic and Pacific oceans. By 1937, she was ready to take on her biggest challenge of all—to become the first person to circumnavigate the globe at the equator. And that's when her fortunes changed.

THE FATAL FLIGHT

On June 1, 1937, Amelia took off from Miami with her navigator, Fred Noonan, heading east around the globe. They completed the first 22,000 miles/35,000 kilometers or so without incident and landed in Lae, New Guinea, on June 29.

The first leg of the remaining 7,000-mile/11,000-kilometer flight over the Pacific—the 2,556 miles/4,113 kilometers to Howland, a tiny coral island barely rising out of the sea—was always going to be dangerous. Contingency plans to aid navigation included regular radio communication with the US Coast Guard vessel *Itasca*, stationed off the island.

Everything was against them. Poor weather conditions made radio communication difficult and celestial navigation impossible; and it emerged later that their charts were almost certainly inaccurate, causing them to search for the island in the wrong location. At 7:42am on July 3, *Itasca* received this message: "We must be on you, but we cannot see you. Fuel is running low. Been unable to reach you by radio. We are flying at 1,000 feet [300 meters]." After that—nothing. *Itasca* began an immediate search, soon joined by a massive and costly rescue mission of ships and aircraft authorized by President Franklin D.

"Flying may not be all plain sailing, but the fun of it is worth the price." —*Amelia Earhart*

Fatal flight. *Amelia assembles her luggage in preparation for her circumnavigation of the globe in 1937. She could not know that she would never return.*

Roosevelt, which ended unsuccessfully on July 19. Amelia's husband launched his own search, not conceding defeat until October. With no body to confirm her fate, Amelia was declared legally dead on January 5, 1939.

Amelia at one with her plane. *Pictured in February 1937. The fact that her aircraft became an extension of herself makes her failure to complete her flight safely all the more mysterious.*

DROWNED OR CASTAWAY?

Amelia's whereabouts have proved a tantalizing topic, and among those still seeking the truth is The International Group for Historic Aircraft Recovery (TIGHAR). Their hypothesis is that she did not plunge into the Pacific near Howland Island, but instead landed safely some 350 miles/560 kilometers southeast on the uninhabited island of Nikumaroro (formerly Gardner Island), lived as a castaway, and died there. Among the more inconclusive artifacts that suggest her presence on the atoll, such as tools and fragments of clothing, is what TIGHAR believe is the real clue—a sheet of battered aluminum studded with rivet holes, thought to be a repair patch from the plane. Cynics argue that search planes scoured the entire area, including Gardner Island, at the time of Amelia's disappearance, but TIGHAR are not so easily dissuaded, believing that the Electra lies in deep water off the island's west end—and that the partial skeleton of a castaway, found by a British Colonial Service officer in 1940 and believed at the time to be male and thus forgotten, was in fact that of Amelia Earhart.

The conspiracy theory

Among the theories that abounded after Amelia's disappearance, the most popular and enduring is that she was actually acting as a US spy on an intelligence-gathering mission and was captured, along with Noonan, by the Japanese, never to be seen again.

ANTOINE DE SAINT-EXUPÉRY

In July 1944, a valiant pilot took off on a reconnaissance mission, and when he failed to return the news spread fast, for this was no ordinary flier—this was the widely acclaimed author Antoine de Saint-Exupéry. France's great national treasure had vanished, and it was to be more than fifty years before his silver identity bracelet, discovered by chance, would give a clue to his fate.

Antoine Marie Jean-Baptiste Roger, Vicomte de Saint Exupéry
Born: June 29, 1900, Lyon, France
Spouse: Consuelo (m. 1931)
Died: July 31, 1944, Marseille, France

ANTOINE DE SAINT-EXUPÉRY was born into a very old French aristocratic family, which after the death of his father was reduced to an impoverished state—but all things are relative, and Saint-Exupéry's childhood home was a chateau and his early life one of freedom and privilege. At the age of 12, he had an opportunity that very few young boys would have been offered in the early 1900s—he took his first trip in an airplane, and fell in love with flying.

ANTOINE TAKES OFF

Saint-Exupéry was educated first in France and then at boarding school in Switzerland, but surprisingly for a man who would write one of the world's best-loved books and receive numerous literary awards, he was not a good student. He twice failed the entrance examination to the École Navale, France's naval officer academy; he then studied architecture at the prestigious École des Beaux-Arts in Paris, but left without graduating. Perhaps he knew deep down that his destiny was to "till the skies."

In 1921, while carrying out his compulsory military service, Saint-Exupéry took private flying lessons, realizing a dream he'd harbored since that magical first flight. The following year he transferred to the Air Force and received his wings, but it was a brief stint—he resigned after fracturing his skull in his first crash, as his fiancée's family wanted their future son-in-law in one piece. The couple broke up soon afterward, and in 1926 Saint-Exupéry became a mail pilot for Aéropostale, covering routes between France, Spain, and North Africa—a brave career choice at a time when navigational technology was at its most basic. Part of his brief was to negotiate the safe release of pilots who had crashed in the Sahara and been taken

Author, aviator, aristocrat. *Antoine de Saint-Exupéry used his lifelong love of flying as inspiration for his written works.*

Homecoming hero. *Saint-Exupéry returns to France aboard the* Kawsar *after a near-death experience in the Sahara in December 1935. His wife, Consuelo, a writer and artist, is at his side.*

hostage by local Moorish tribes; such was his diplomacy in the task that he was awarded a Légion d'honneur, the highest French civilian award. In 1929, he was transferred to Argentina to help establish that country's airmail system.

But Saint-Exupéry's aeronautical exploits sometimes led him into difficulties. In December 1935, Antoine and his navigator were attempting to break the speed record in an air race from Paris to Saigon. The prize money of 150,000 French francs (equivalent to around $175,000 today) was not to be theirs, however—they crashed in the Sahara and would have died of dehydration had they not been rescued by a passing Bedouin on a camel. But Saint-Exupéry took everything in his stride, because, in his words, "Writing is the fruit of experience"—and his experiences provided sumptuous fruit for writing, his second love.

THE WORDSMITH PILOT

Like most successful authors, Saint-Exupéry wrote about what he knew—and in his case, this meant writing about pilots. He even wrote as he was flying, scattering his drafts and drawings around his feet. His first story, *The Aviator*, was published in a magazine in 1925 and four years later he published his first novel, *Southern Mail*, celebrating the courage of pilots. After his return from Argentina in 1931, he published *Night Flight*, inspired by his adventures in the air over South America. This was to become his first major success, for which he was awarded the Prix Fémina literary prize for the best novel published that year. His 1939 memoir, *Wind, Sand and Stars*, was an account of his unintentional four-day sojourn in the Sahara after his crash in the 1935 air race. For this, he won the Académie Française Grand Prize for Novel Writing and the US National Book Award; but the best was yet to come.

Asteroid B-612

An asteroid discovered in 1993 was named 46610 "Bésixdouze" (B-612) after the little prince's tiny home planet. His creator also has an asteroid named after him: 2578 Saint-Exupéry, discovered in 1975.

LE PETIT PRINCE

In October 1942, Saint-Exupéry wrote and illustrated the children's fable for adults for which he is most well-known—Le Petit Prince, the tale of a pilot stranded in the desert who meets a small, golden-haired, planet-hopping boy from the fictitious asteroid B-612. Both characters are essentially Saint-Exupéry himself and the story addresses his own profound existential anxieties; the little prince learns from a friendly fox the important lesson that "It is only with the heart that one can see rightly; what is essential is invisible to the eye."

The book was published in the United States early the following year, in both French and English (as The Little Prince), although not in France until 1946—most of the main publishing houses had all but shut down during the wartime German occupation, and in any case all manuscripts were subject to German censorship. Le Petit Prince has been translated into many languages and is estimated to have sold more copies than any book except the Bible; it has also inspired television series, radio and stage plays, ballets, operas, and, most recently, an animated film. There is even a museum dedicated to the story in Hakone, Japan. The original 140-page draft of the book—coffee-stained and studded with cigarette burns—is now held by The Morgan Library & Museum in Manhattan, New York, along with several watercolor illustrations of the narrative.

Le Petit Prince (The Little Prince). *Like many children's books, it has a philosophical theme and appeals as much to adults as it does to their offspring.*

THE TALE OF THE ROSE

In order to understand Le Petit Prince, and indeed Saint-Exupéry himself, it is first necessary to become acquainted with the third love in his life—his flamboyant and capricious Salvadoran wife, Consuelo, whom he met in Buenos Aires in 1930 and fell in love with at first sight. He immediately announced his intention to marry her and indeed he did, in France, in 1931. Theirs was a tempestuous marriage, reflected in the relationship between the little prince of Saint-Exupéry's imagination and the beautiful, thorny rose that he could neither live with, nor live without; Saint-Exupéry abandoned Consuelo constantly, and then yearned for her, exactly as the little prince did with his beloved rose. Consuelo wrote an account of her stormy life with Saint-Exupéry but, apparently not intending to publish the manuscript, she locked it away in a trunk, where it was discovered fifteen years after her death in 1979, along with love letters from Saint-Exupéry. It was published as The Tale of the Rose in France in 2000, the 100th anniversary of Saint-Exupéry's birth, and became an instant bestseller.

"The Little Prince will shine upon children with a sidewise gleam. It will strike them in some place that is not the mind and glow there until the time comes for them to comprehend it." —P.L. *Travers, author of* Mary Poppins

NEW YORK SOJOURN

When Saint-Exupéry wrote *Le Petit Prince*, he was living with Consuelo in New York. Britain and France had declared war on Germany in 1939 and Saint-Exupéry became a military reconnaissance pilot with the Free French air force—he was too old to fly fighter planes and flatly refused to fly a bomber—until the German occupation of France began in May of the following year. With the fall of France, he went into exile in the United States. He was one of many—it was not safe for members of the cultural elite to remain in France and, for the moment at least, it was business as usual in America. But that was to change when the US entered the war after the bombing of Pearl Harbor in 1941. When Saint-Exupéry published another top-ten bestseller, *Flight to Arras*, in 1942, he demonstrated his diplomatic skills once again when he presented a copy to the American president with the inscription: "For President Roosevelt, whose country is assuming the immense task of saving the world."

> "I, who do not know how to draw, have created the most beautiful drawing in the world."
> —*Antoine de Saint-Exupéry*

THE FINAL FLIGHT

In 1943, Saint-Exupéry published another book, *Letter to a Hostage*, dedicated to his forty million countrymen living under Nazi oppression. That year, he rejoined his squadron in North Africa, and learned to fly the Lockheed P-38 Lightning fighter aircraft. It was a brave move, or perhaps foolish—his body was broken and in constant pain from injuries sustained in numerous plane crashes. He was also suffering from depression; he had been devastated by the occupation of France, many of his old flying comrades had been killed, and he had felt isolated in the US. But Saint-Exupéry, with his aristocratic background and personal beliefs, had a strong sense of duty and sacrifice for the greater good, themes that appeared in his writing and his own actions; what else could he do but fight for his country?

On July 31, 1944, Saint-Exupéry took off from the island of Corsica; it was the nearest he came to setting foot on French soil after his return from America. He was on a reconnaissance mission ahead of Operation Dragoon, the planned Allied invasion of southern France that would play a vital role in the country's liberation the following month. He did not return.

Flying—his first love. *Saint-Exupéry with a fellow pilot, photographed in 1929. The experiences of those with whom he worked in the mail service became a theme in his novels.*

ANOTHER DELIBERATE FAILURE?

When neither Saint-Exupéry nor his plane were found, he was officially deemed to have been killed in action, shot down by enemy fire as he headed toward the French coast. But there were some who believed that years earlier, the youthful Saint-Exupéry had deliberately failed his École Navale entrance examination, and now there was speculation that he had deliberately crashed his plane, overcome by feelings of pessimism about the future.

Many years later, in 1998, a French fisherman working just off the coast of Marseille snared a silver identity bracelet in his net. It bore the name Antoine de Saint-Exupéry, along with his wife's name in parentheses and the address of his New York publisher. It was the first clue ever found as to his fate, and an emotive discovery for the French, for whom Saint-Exupéry had long represented heroism, adventure, and poetry. It also offered new scope for discovering his whereabouts, and two years later a scuba diver found the partial remains of a Lockheed P-38 Lightning scattered over a wide area nearby. When an underwater salvage team brought the wreckage to the surface, the serial number confirmed that it was Saint-Exupéry's plane. However, the remains of the man himself were nowhere to be found.

A clue to his fate. *The weathered silver identity bracelet that provided a vital clue as to Saint-Exupéry's fate. It is thought to have been a gift from his American publishers.*

"I SHOT DOWN SAINT-EXUPÉRY"

No bullet holes were found in the recovered wreckage and it was concluded that the mystery of why the plane came down on a perfectly clear day would never be solved. However, in 2008, Horst Rippert, an 88-year-old former Luftwaffe pilot, confessed his fears that he might have been responsible for Saint-Exupéry's demise. He reported that on the day Saint-Exupéry disappeared, he saw a P-38 Lightning flying below him, went after it, and shot it down. He was unable to see the pilot, but stated that even with a clear view he would not have been able to identify him. When the news broke that Saint-Exupéry was missing, Rippert hoped, and continued to hope throughout his life, that the pilot he brought down was not the author whose books he had read in his youth, and loved.

So if Rippert's story were true, the mystery of how Saint-Exupéry died has been solved— leaving just one loose end still untied. Sometime after his disappearance, a Frenchwoman reported having seen a plane crash near the Bay of Carqueiranne off Toulon, to the east of Marseille, and in September 1944 an unidentifiable body in French colors was discovered and buried in Carqueiranne. Little notice was taken because it was not in the crash site area, but could it be that his body had been swept away from the wrecked plane and along the coast— has Antoine, Vicomte de Saint-Exupéry been safely at rest in a small Provençal harbor town all along?

The mysterious number
The little prince was known to love sunsets, and they are mentioned forty-four times in the book. Saint-Exupéry flew into a sunset over the Mediterranean Sea in 1944, and was never seen again. And finally, his age at the time of his disappearance? Forty-four, of course.

GLENN MILLER

On December 15, 1944, a Norseman aircraft took off from a British Royal Air Force base. It was carrying an illustrious passenger—the hugely popular American bandleader, Glenn Miller. His destination was Paris, recently liberated from Nazi occupation, where he was to entertain the troops at Christmas. But Miller mysteriously disappeared over the English Channel and was never seen again.

Alton Glenn Miller
Born: March 1, 1904, Clarinda, Iowa, US
Spouse: Helen Burger (m. 1928)
Children: Steven (adopted 1943); Jonnie (adopted 1944)
Died: December 15, 1944, English Channel
Buried: At sea

THE ROUSING CONTRIBUTION a brass band makes in times of conflict was first exploited in the American Civil War, when regimental bands on both sides played at rallies to promote enlistment. The dances popular at that time were the polka, galop, quadrille, and waltz. Eighty years later, there was a different style of war, a different style of music, and a different style of dance—swing. Glenn Miller's style.

"He just played on that horn all the time." —*Mattie Lou Miller*

SETTING THE SCENE

Miller was born in a small rural town in Iowa, but the family moved state several times during his upbringing, and each new location took him further along the path to stardom. The first move was to Tryon, Nebraska, where Miller's mother, Mattie Lou, played the pump organ to entertain her two young sons on long evenings on their homestead, and his father, Lewis, bought him his first musical instrument—a mandolin, which Miller promptly swapped for a horn. "He just played on that horn all the time," Mattie Lou recalled later. "It got to where Pop and I used to wonder if he'd ever amount to anything." How needlessly they worried about his future!

From Nebraska, the family moved to Grant City, Missouri, where Miller played the trombone in the community band. After that was Fort Morgan, Colorado, where Miller went to high school and became interested in a new musical genre—dance band music. The style originated in New Orleans, the traditional home of jazz, and was essentially the relaxation of structured band music by African-American musicians, who became masters of the art of improvisation and created a whole new sound. White musicians adopted the style and bands such as The Original Dixieland Jazz Band—the first to record jazz commercially—introduced it to New York. The cheerful rhythms were just what was needed at the end of World War I, when the world was feeling jaded.

Horn player extraordinaire. *Bandleader Glenn Miller with his favorite instrument. As a young boy, he milked cows to earn money to buy his first trombone.*

Glenn Miller and his Orchestra. *Performing for the Chesterfield radio show in the early 1940s. Live broadcasts, reaching a wide audience, were Miller's route to success.*

Miller was captivated by the sound, and experimented with it in a band formed with like-minded classmates. In 1923, after graduation, he signed with a Dixieland group called Senter's Sentapeeds, and was on his way to realizing his ambition to become a professional musician. He enrolled in the University of Colorado but discovered he really had no time to spare for studying, and left to concentrate on music. For over a decade he worked with a number of different musicians, including famous names such as Benny Goodman and the Dorsey Brothers, first in Los Angeles and Chicago, and then in New York. He also studied with a music theorist, Joseph Schillinger. His knowledge was expanding rapidly—as music arranger, player, and band leader.

"A band ought to have a sound of its own; it ought to have a personality." *—Glenn Miller*

GLENN MILLER AND HIS ORCHESTRA

In 1937, and now aged 33, Miller decided it was time to take the plunge and set up his own orchestra, the Glenn Miller Band. It was not a success, and played its last date on January 2 the following year. But Miller had learned a lot, and realized that he needed to find a way to make jazz less about the musicians demonstrating their skill and more about appealing to the listener. He assembled another orchestra and this time he found the magic formula, the distinctive big band "sound" that made his music unique and memorable—a clarinet lead, supported by four saxophones and vocalists. Later, he added trombone and trumpet to the wind-section mix.

Miller quickly proved that success begets success. Some of the venues where the orchestra played, such as the Glen Island Casino in New York, broadcast live on national radio, enabling Miller to reach a far wider audience. The orchestra's live appearances began to break attendance records, and Miller was signed for his own radio show. It was the fall of 1939; war had been declared in Europe on September 1, but the United States was not engaged in the conflict. Pearl Harbor was yet to come.

IN THE MOOD

Meanwhile, Glen Miller and His Orchestra were becoming highly successful recording artists, with many of the tunes written by Miller himself. He opened and closed his radio performances with the mellow "Moonlight Serenade," while live performances often ended with his most famous song, "In the Mood," which was recorded on August 1, 1939, and held the number one slot in the charts for thirty weeks. Other recordings, now considered swing classics, included "Tuxedo Junction," "Pennsylvania 6-5000," and "Chattanooga Choo Choo." The latter was the band's biggest seller at 1.2 million copies, and Miller was awarded the first ever gold record. But it was now February 1942; the naval base at Pearl Harbor been attacked by Japanese fighter planes two months earlier, and the US was at war.

"In the Mood." The sheet music cover for one of the orchestra's most famous numbers. It references the "jitterbug craze" that lightened the war years in the US and beyond.

THE BAND IS DISBANDED

Miller, now 38, was too old to be drafted so, determined to do his bit, he gave up his extremely lucrative orchestra and volunteered for service. The navy turned down his application, but he was accepted by the army after some skillful cajoling. He asked to be put in charge of a modernized army band "to put a little more spring into the feet of our marching men and a little more joy into their hearts." The civilian orchestra's final rendering of "Moonlight Serenade" at a concert in Passaic, New Jersey, on September 27, 1942, was more melancholy than mellow.

Miller in uniform, a true patriot. *Before his mysterious disappearance in December 1944, the fifty-member Glenn Miller Army Air Force Band gave more than eight hundred performances to boost morale.*

MILLER DONS A UNIFORM

Miller was appointed a captain in the Army Specialists Corps, and redirected his considerable energies into fund-raising for the war effort and hosting a weekly radio broadcast, I *Sustain the Wings*, designed to attract new Air Corps recruits. Most importantly, he created a new fifty-member band. In the summer of 1944, Miller took the band to England to entertain the troops live. After a brief stay in London, where only fortunate timing prevented the entire band being killed by a German V-I buzz bomb, they moved to the town of Bedford, north of the capital.

MISSING IN ACTION

During the war, many entertainers—including Miller—flew to and from the RAF training base Twinwood, located just outside Bedford, north of London, where the British Broadcasting Corporation (BBC) had its wartime headquarters. On December 15, 1944, at Twinwood, Miller boarded a single-engine Noorduyn Norseman aircraft, bound for Paris to organize a Christmas broadcast for the troops who had liberated the city. It was the last flight he would ever take; the plane crashed into the English Channel, and the wreckage was never recovered.

Why this happened has long been a matter of conjecture. Inevitably, there were conspiracy theories—that Miller was assassinated while engaged in a secret plot to overthrow Hitler; that he returned secretly to the US, sick but alive; that he made it to Paris and was found dead in a brothel. Another suggestion was that he was a victim of friendly fire, his plane destroyed by a bomb jettisoned by one of over a hundred aircraft returning to England after an aborted Allied raid, although US Army Air Force records indicate that the timings make that impossible.

ICED UP

In 2014, Dennis Spragg, senior consultant to the Glenn Miller Archive at the University of Colorado Boulder, Miller's alma mater, announced that he had found the answer in long-forgotten military documents. There was a thick fog on the fateful day and the plane was flying low over the water because of the poor visibility. Ice formed, freezing the mechanics and causing the plane to crash. The low altitude would have allowed the pilot virtually no time to react—and in any case, he was not certified for flying by instruments alone.

The fact that the military did not announce Miller's disappearance until December 24 appears to compound the mystery, but in fact they very quickly drew their conclusion about the cause of the crash, and the outcome. It was simply not their policy at the time to release such information, leaving Miller's millions of grieving fans in ignorance of his fate. So it seems the mystery is solved—but for one curious factor. In 2012, a notebook was discovered belonging to an amateur plane spotter, Richard Anderton. On December 15, 1944, the 17-year-old Anderton recorded that he had sighted a Norseman, almost certainly Miller's, to the west of London, so it was not on the expected route. Was the inexperienced pilot merely lost in the fog—or was Miller's destination not Paris at all?

The band played on
The band presented the Christmas concert under the direction of another conductor, and continued to perform for the remainder of the war, playing their final concert for President Harry S. Truman on November 13, 1945.

Memorial gravestone. *Grove Street Cemetery, New Haven, Connecticut, where Miller made personal appearances during the war. It was placed at the head of the (empty) plot in 1998.*

HAROLD HOLT

On the surface it was a depressingly familiar tale: a middle-aged man had drowned after unwisely going swimming in a very heavy sea at a popular Australian beach. But many thought that this was no ordinary accident: The story of the prime minster of Australia's disappearance quickly became mired in a dense network of rumors and conspiracy theories, some of which still persist fifty years on.

Harold Edward Holt
Born: August 5, 1908, Stanmore, New South Wales, Australia
Spouse: Zara Fell (m. 1946)
Disappeared: December 17, 1967, Cheviot Beach, near Portsea, Victoria, Australia
Pronounced dead: December 19, 1967

HAROLD HOLT had only been prime minister for just under two years when he disappeared—but his political life had already lasted for more than three decades. Born in Sydney, he was educated in Melbourne before training as a lawyer and serving at the Bar for several years. He stood for parliament as candidate for the United Australia Party, for the seat of Fawkner, in the state of Victoria, in 1935, and won, holding the seat for the next four elections, subsequently winning another eight as the representative for Higgins, also in Victoria.

RISE TO POWER

In 1940, Holt briefly became minister for labor and national service, then served on the back benches for three years before becoming a founding member of Australia's new Liberal Party in 1944. When the Liberals came into government as part of a coalition in 1949, he was put back in charge of his previous ministry, but with the addition of immigration, an important post after World War II, when immigration to Australia was at its height. He was appointed Leader of the House of Representatives and deputy Liberal leader in 1956, then Treasurer in 1958—in which role he dealt with a recession two years later. He finally became prime minister when his predecessor, Robert Menzies, retired at the end of January 1966.

AUSTRALIA'S ANSWER TO JOHN F. KENNEDY

Holt's friends and supporters attested to his charisma: He was a lively conversationalist, a keen sportsman, particularly fond of swimming and diving, and, allegedly, a magnet for women. The popular press made much of both his personal and his political appeal, similar, they said, to that of JFK in the United States. Holt married Zara Fell, an old flame, in 1946: They had dated but broken up while still students, and Zara had married James Fell, a captain in the British Army. When she and Fell divorced, Zara and Holt rekindled their relationship; on

Sydney International Airport, 1966. *Prime Minister Harold Holt waves as he boards a plane for Singapore. He would disappear just a year later.*

St Kilda Town Hall, Melbourne, c. 1953. *Holt and his wife, Zara, take to the floor. Zara traveled with Holt often, but was in Canberra on the day he disappeared.*

their marriage, Holt also adopted the three sons she had had with Fell. The two of them made a lively pairing: Zara was energetic and spirited, well able to manage her relationship with the charming, flirtatious Holt and to play the part of Australia's first lady with ease.

"I KNOW THIS BEACH LIKE THE BACK OF MY HAND …"

Holt and his family kept a weekend cottage at Portsea, a popular resort near Melbourne, and on December 17, 1967, he went there to spend some time without his wife. Officially he was just taking a day or two out, and they would both be there the following week to celebrate Christmas with the family—unofficially, he was seeing a girlfriend and neighbor, Marjorie Gillespie. He collected her in his Pontiac and they set off for the beach in the late morning, along with Gillespie's daughter, Vyner, Vyner's boyfriend, and Alan Stewart, another family friend.

The first beach the party arrived at was closed, due to the high winds and water swell. Determined to swim, Holt drove to nearby Cheviot Beach, which was not patrolled. Vyner would later comment on the rough seas in her police statement, but Holt unhesitatingly waded out into the water. Martin Simpson, Vyner's boyfriend, made to follow him, but stopped when he was knee deep, feeling the pull of the undercurrent. Alan Stewart did the same. In his statement, he was to say that Holt had swum into "dangerous turbulence." From the beach, the seething water looked as though it was boiling.

Spear fishing, 1966. *The prime minister, seen here in mask and wetsuit, loved the sport and would sometimes take risks to secure a catch.*

As the party watched, Holt vanished from sight. His companions walked up to a rocky vantage point from where they could look down on the sea, but they still couldn't spot him. Within minutes, Stewart had run to find help and by the time the rescue services arrived, local scuba divers were already out in the surf looking for Holt. It was a fine, blowy day and, hearing the news, more and more people started to arrive. By sundown there were two hundred people on the beach, including members of the coast guard service, the army, and the navy. Helicopters were circling overhead, but those on board could see no sign of Holt. Despite the massive rescue effort, his body would never be found.

PRESUMED DEAD

Two days after his disappearance the Australian government issued a statement declaring that Holt was "presumed dead" (although the sea search, the largest ever undertaken in Australia, would go on for another three weeks). The conspiracy theories followed quickly on this news, although not before an

Cheviot Beach, Victoria, Australia. *Holt waded out into the turbulent sea from this beach on December 17, 1967, and was never seen again.*

Baffling. *Marjorie Gillespie (right), Holt's girlfriend, points to the place where she last saw the prime minister in December 1967. This annotated aerial photograph (below) shows the area from which Holt went missing.*

THE RIP

POINT NEPEAN

CHEVIOT BEACH

MR HOLT LOST HERE

TO PORTSEA

Indian swami had contacted the Australian High Commission to say that he had seen the body of Holt resting on the seabed in a vision. Divers searched the alleged spot but found nothing.

A memorial service was held on December 22, attended by Lyndon Johnson, the presidents of both Vietnam and South Korea, the British prime minister, and a young Prince Charles, heir to the British throne. The search, however, was still taking place—it wasn't called off until well into the New Year.

Some held that Holt had actually committed suicide, although even those in favor of this theory admitted that it was unlikely that he would do so in clear sight of a group of friends—and few supported the idea that he had seemed depressed. Quite a few of the huge number of communications sent to everyone from the government to the rescue services alleged alien abduction, and these were unsurprisingly dismissed straight away. Another theory, not much less incredible, involved the CIA.

> "He wasn't a young man any more. I think he fell for his own publicity. He believed he could not drown." —*Lawrence Newell,*
>
> *the police inspector who led the search for Holt*

"ALL THE WAY WITH LBJ"

Why would the CIA have wanted Holt gone? One of his more controversial policies had been his support of Lyndon B. Johnson in the war in Vietnam. He was well-known for a speech in 1966 in which he vouched that he would go "all the way with LBJ," and he had committed more than six thousand troops to serve with the Americans. There had been recent signs that popular support for the war was waning fast, though— had the CIA decided to dispatch Holt before he opted to pull Australia out of Vietnam? Examined objectively, it was a wild idea—Holt had shown no signs of withdrawing his support—and, in any case, how would the CIA have managed it? Could divers have been waiting to drag Holt to his death in rough seas? It seemed spectacularly unlikely.

This was not as unlikely, though, as the theory that was to be posed by the British journalist Anthony Grey in 1983. In his book, *The Prime Minister was a Spy*, he posited that Holt had been a spy for the Chinese government for his entire political life. Threatened with exposure, Grey claimed, Holt had made his escape—and been picked up by Chinese divers who had spirited him to a submarine waiting for him just outside the bay. Zara Holt had a characteristically trenchant response to this outlandish account: "Chinese submarine?" she scoffed, "He didn't even like Chinese food."

Rumors, though, persisted for years. In 2005, a coroner's inquiry in Victoria found that Holt had drowned in rough seas, and that the fate of his body was unknown, although there were plenty of sharks in the area. Six months earlier, Holt had had a narrow escape in the same spot when snorkeling and had had to be helped to shore, and at the time of his disappearance he was being treated for a shoulder injury that could have affected how strongly he could swim. Holt's disappearance in the ocean he loved so much has now become part of Australia's national myth.

"We've always believed the death was purely accidental. There was nothing sinister about it ... (the coroner's enquiry) might put a stop to silly rumors about Chinese submarines." —Sam Holt, *Holt's stepson, commenting on the 2005 coroner's inquiry*

Holt and Lyndon B. Johnson. *Holt was a staunch supporter of the US president's actions in Vietnam.*

LORD LUCAN

At about 9:45pm on November 7, 1974, Veronica, Countess of Lucan, staggered into The Plumbers Arms, a pub in London's exclusive Belgravia district. She was covered in blood and clearly in a state of shock. Drinkers in the bar claimed they had heard her shouting "My children, my children … He's killed the nanny …"

Richard John Bingham, Seventh Earl of Lucan
Born: December 18, 1934, Marylebone, London
Spouse: Veronica Mary Duncan (m. November 20, 1963)
Children: Frances (b. 1964), George (b. 1967), Camilla (b. 1970)
Disappeared: November 7, 1974, date of death unknown

LADY LUCAN was taken to hospital; when police went to check the family home at 46 Lower Belgrave Street, they found the body of Sandra Rivett, the Lucan children's nanny, beaten about the head and roughly stuffed into a sack lying in the doorway of the basement kitchen. Nearby was a length of lead pipe wrapped in bandages, which were sodden with blood.

"BELGRAVIA MURDER—EARL SOUGHT"

It was tabloid gold, a story that had everything: a gambling-mad aristocrat, a wronged wife, innocent children, mistaken identity, and a murder, plus all the trappings of high society. The press showed no restraint as the details began to emerge. By November 8 the bare facts— that a woman had been bludgeoned to death, that the Countess of Lucan claimed that it was her husband who was the murderer, and that Lord Lucan himself had disappeared—were being widely reported, along with plenty of speculation. And for the police, one of the largest, longest, and most frustrating manhunts in British history had begun.

A TROUBLED MARRIAGE

Lucan, then Lord Bingham, had been educated at Eton, one of the UK's most famous and exclusive independent boarding schools, before joining the Coldstream Guards, the oldest British Army regiment in continuous active service. From there, he took up a career in merchant banking for a brief spell, leaving regular employment for good in 1960. He was tall, extremely handsome in a rather old-fashioned style, and a keen sportsman. By the time he met Veronica Duncan, he was also a professional gambler—his departure from the working world had been triggered by a win of £26,000 (worth around half a million dollars today) in a single forty-eight-hour session of the card game chemin de fer at Le Touquet in France, after which he was also known by the nickname "Lucky" Lucan. It was ironic that thereafter such extraordinary strokes of luck seemed to desert him—he regularly lost large sums and was invariably short of money.

John Bingham, Seventh Earl of Lucan. *Photographed with Veronica Duncan in 1963, the couple were celebrating the occasion of their engagement.*

Lucan first met Veronica through her sister Christina and brother-in-law, William Shand Kydd, a wealthy businessman, in 1963. The two soon married and just two months after the wedding Lucan's father died and he inherited the earldom. The Duncans were a military family, and Veronica was quiet, artistic, and slightly shy. Once married, she found it hard to acclimatize to her new husband's world: evenings were spent at the tables playing chemin de fer, poker, or perhaps backgammon (Lucan favored games of skill over games of pure chance). His usual haunt was the Clermont Club in London's Berkeley Square, owned by the eccentric businessman John Aspinall, himself an enthusiastic gambler, and attended by such live-hard, play-hard society figures as the financier James Goldsmith and the Conservative politician Lord Boothby. Play went on into the small hours, and Veronica could watch from the sidelines or go home alone. Her rather reserved personality, too, didn't fit easily with the louche big spenders of the Lucan set.

The couple's first child, Frances, was born late in 1964, and was followed by George in 1967 and Camilla in 1970. Veronica suffered from postnatal depression after each birth and, from finding her a bore, Lucan now began to say she was

Lady Lucan with Frances and George, *two of her three children. When Veronica and Lucan separated, there were many points of dispute, but the one that both felt most strongly about was who should have custody.*

mad. In 1971, he tried to persuade her to become an in-patient at a psychiatric hospital, but she refused. By the end of 1972 the marriage had broken down irretrievably and Lucan moved out, taking a flat in Eaton Row, near the family home so that he could see his children regularly.

LEAD-UP TO TRAGEDY

In the two years between the separation and Lucan's disappearance, relations between the couple became bitter and acrimonious. Lucan may not have been a responsible husband, but everyone who knew him agreed that he adored his children and, convinced of his wife's instability, he was set on gaining custody. He hired private detectives to spy on Veronica and the children in the hope of finding her unfit to care for them; on one occasion he even had them made wards of court, abducting them as they returned from school. Veronica was forced to defend her mental state in court, but was eventually awarded custody—the judge noting that she suffered from depression but was not mentally ill.

Lucan, by now in such severe financial straits that he was facing bankruptcy, and allowed to see his children for only two weekends a month, was becoming desperate. He talked to any of his friends who would listen about his determination to win his children back, combining requests to borrow money with intemperate threats against his wife.

Veronica Lucan employed a series of nannies over 1973 and 1974, a time when nannying for the Lucan children had become increasingly stressful, as it could never be certain what Lucan would try next. He made unnerving telephone calls to Lower Belgrave Street, disguising his voice and asking to speak to people who didn't live there or simply waiting in silence until the person hung up. He would intercept the children when they were out, or have them followed by detectives looking for signs that they weren't being cared for properly.

After a series of temporary nannies had come and gone, at the end of August 1974 Sandra Rivett arrived. She got along well with Lady Lucan—Sandra, too, had had a failed marriage and her own little boy lived with her parents. Veronica Lucan remembered her as "a kind, loyal and dignified woman," and the children quickly became fond of her.

Sandra Rivett. *Photographed shortly before she was killed. She was 29 at the time of her murder, and had worked at Lower Belgrave Street for just a few months. Sandra was popular with both Lady Lucan and her children.*

THE MURDER

On the evening of November 7, her two youngest children already in bed, Lady Lucan was watching television with Frances and Sandra Rivett. It was Thursday, usually Sandra's evening off, but that week she had swapped to a different day. During a break she went down to the basement kitchen to make a cup of tea. When she hadn't come back after twenty minutes, Veronica went to investigate. She turned the switch at the top of the stairs, but no light came on, and as she walked down to the kitchen, she was grabbed by the throat and hit about the head. She fought back, biting, kicking, and screaming; when her attacker told her to shut up, she was horrified to recognize her husband's voice.

Veronica Lucan's subsequent account was accepted by the police and backed up by what they found at the house: She had asked her husband where

Sandra was, and he had admitted to having killed her. Although considerably battered, she had forced herself to remain calm and offered to help him escape. They walked upstairs, Lucan told 9-year-old Frances (who had heard her mother scream) to go to bed, and went to get a towel to help his wife to clean herself up. Seizing the opportunity, Veronica ran out of the house to summon help.

AN INQUIRY BEGINS

By the time the police arrived at Lower Belgrave Street, Lucan had gone. Nor was he at his own flat—over the following twenty-four hours, the police would gradually uncover his movements later that night. He had rung his mother and asked her to collect the children from their home, though without saying where he was. He then drove to Uckfield, south of London, where he called at the house of some of his oldest friends, Ian and Susan Maxwell-Scott, and found Susan at home. He gave her a rambling account of what happened, couching it in the terms of "a terrible accident," and while there, wrote two separate letters to his brother-in-law, William Shand Kydd. One dealt with his money affairs, the second was more personal. In it he described seeing his wife being attacked through the window of the house in Lower Belgrave Street as he passed by, and going to help her. It was an unlikely tale, even more so when police later tested it as a hypothesis and found that the basement area was only visible through a window if the person looking in were on their knees on the pavement. Both letters were stained with blood.

Susan Maxwell-Scott was the last person known to have seen Lucan. He left her at about 1:45am in the morning, and his car was found parked in the port of Newhaven on the English Channel coast, about 15 miles/25 kilometers from Uckfield, the next day. There was no sign of Lucan himself, but bloodstains in the car were matched to the blood of both Sandra Rivett and Veronica Lucan, and a second lead pipe, also wrapped in bandages, was found in the boot.

> "Lucan ... gambled on successfully killing his wife. But when it went terribly wrong he must have realized he only had two options open to him: hand himself in, or kill himself."
>
> —James Wilson, *member of the Clermont Club and friend of Lucan*

From Goa to New Zealand: the men who weren't Lord Lucan

Detectives have flown all over the world following Lucan "leads." Many have been extraordinarily unlikely.

In 2003, for example, a bearded, shambling figure who scratched a living on a Goan beach was "unmasked" as Lucan by Duncan McLaughlin, a former Scotland Yard detective. The only problem was his real identity: he was Barry Halpin, a former folk singer from St Helens, Lancashire, in northern England. McLaughlin had got it risibly wrong.

Four years later, in New Zealand, a man named Roger Woodgate was also reported as being the missing peer. Challenged by a posse of journalists and speaking from the Land Rover in which he was living, his pet possum Redfern beside him, Woodgate firmly denied it, pointing out that not only was he 5 inches/12 centimeters too short to be Lucan, but also a decade too young.

In charge of the case, Detective Chief Superintendent Roy Ranson questioned many of Lucan's friends and associates exhaustively but without really gaining any solid leads. The earl's friends closed ranks, sometimes affecting a superior attitude when questioned or, worse, being flippant—Lady Osborne, mother of John Aspinall who, in addition to owning the Clermont Club, also kept an extensive private zoo, told one exasperated police officer that the last she had heard, Lucan "was being fed to my son's tigers." There were far more questions than there were answers—why had the car been left in Newhaven? Had the earl escaped to France? Or drowned himself, jumping from the English Channel ferry? Or was it a false trail—had his powerful friends spirited him out of the country by some other means? Lucan's own passport and personal belongings were all found at his flat; nothing was missing.

A day in the life. *Lord Lucan, center right, at the card table. He was a member of several upmarket gaming clubs and, despite his "Lucky" nickname, was facing bankruptcy at the time of his sudden disappearance.*

The full inquest into the death of Sandra Rivett was held in June 1975. The coroner found that she had been murdered, and named Lucan as her murderer. Rivett had been about the same height as Lady Lucan, with the same slim build, and it was believed that her murder had been a case of mistaken identity: he had intended to kill Veronica. For at least a decade afterward, the police remained convinced that an answer would emerge—a body would be found, one of the old Clermont Club group would crack and offer new information, or some brand-new piece of evidence would solve the mystery. But as the years became decades, and literally thousands of sightings of the missing earl were reported in locations ranging from Botswana to Australia, none of them ever checked out.

If Lucan were alive now he would be in his 80s. He was declared legally dead in 1999, but his son was only allowed finally to take his title, becoming George, Eighth Earl of Lucan, in February 2016. Outside court, the new earl made a heartfelt statement: "Our family has no idea how our father met his own end … It is a mystery and it may well remain that way forever … I would ask for everyone to consider [that] a person did die here in terrible circumstances, and a family lost a father."

Poignantly, Sandra Rivett's son, Neil Berriman, who was present to hear Bingham granted his title, also made a statement. "This will not go away," he said, "There is no getting away from the fact that whatever happened that night Lord Lucan is guilty of something in my eyes."

Perhaps John Aspinall got closest to the truth when, shortly after the murder, he told reporters, "I find it difficult to imagine him in Brazil or Haiti as a fugitive. I don't think he has the capacity to adapt." Many of Lucan's friends agreed that, finding himself in a situation that he simply would not have been able to get out of, he had killed himself.

"I would be very grateful if we all moved on and found another Loch Ness monster out there."

—George Bingham, *Eighth Earl of Lucan, February 2016*

JIMMY HOFFA

At around 2:30pm on Wednesday July 30, 1975, Jimmy Hoffa, ex-president of the powerful Teamsters union, made a call to his wife from a payphone at the Machus Red Fox Inn on Telegraph Road in Bloomfield Hills, a northwest suburb of Detroit. It was the last call he would ever make.

James Riddle Hoffa
Born: February 14, 1913, Brazil, Indiana
Spouse: Josephine Poszywak (m. September 24, 1936)
Children: Barbara Ann (b. 1938, m. Robert Crancer); James P. Hoffa, (b. 1941)
Disappeared, believed murdered: July 30, 1975, Bloomfield Hills, Michigan

JOSEPHINE RECALLED that he sounded irritable—he'd been waiting for two associates to turn up for a meeting for nearly a half hour and wanted to know, had anyone called to reschedule or to leave a message? No, his wife told him, she hadn't heard from anyone. He'd be on his way back home then, he said, and hung up. She never heard from him again.

MISSING PERSON #75-3425

What is singular about Hoffa's story was how quickly "missing" became "missing, presumed dead." When someone goes missing, the first question the police ask is usually whether anyone might have wanted to harm them. Hoffa was unusual—far from needing to establish possible suspects, the police were spoiled for choice. Missing person #75-3425 had a complicated history, and it had made him plenty of enemies. While his personal life was straightforward—a devoted husband and father who lived in modest circumstances and drove a smart but unshowy Pontiac—his past as President of Teamsters, the circumstances in which he had lost that role, and his subsequent efforts to regain it all ensured that he knew plenty of people who habitually operated on the wrong side of the law.

Despite his son Jimmy Junior's naïve—or disingenuous—public statement that he could think of no one who would have wished his father harm, the FBI knew otherwise. From the day of his disappearance, their assumption was that this had been a classic Mafia hit.

ALL-AMERICAN BOY

Jimmy Hoffa's early history was pure blue-collar striver. He was born in Indiana to poor parents and his father, a coal driller, died when he was just seven years old. Four years later, his mother relocated the family to Detroit, where Hoffa was enrolled in the local elementary school. By the age of 14 he had left formal education, keen to start earning and helping at home, and was soon unloading railway cars of produce for a chain of grocery stores for 32 cents an hour. He took to negotiation with the ease of a natural, and while in that job organized his first labor strike, persuading his work colleagues to stop unloading perishable

At the height of his power. *Jimmy Hoffa pictured outside the Teamsters' offices in Washington, DC, in April 1959.*

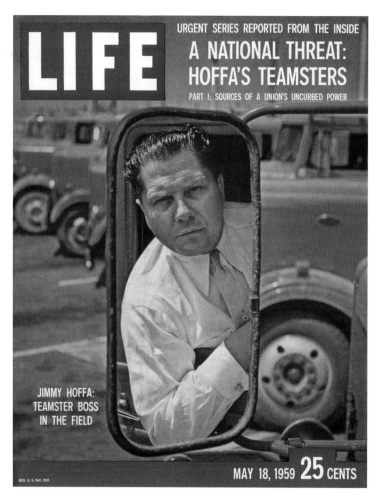

URGENT SERIES REPORTED FROM THE INSIDE

LIFE

A NATIONAL THREAT:
HOFFA'S TEAMSTERS

PART I: SOURCES OF A UNION'S UNCURBED POWER

JIMMY HOFFA:
TEAMSTER BOSS
IN THE FIELD

MAY 18, 1959 **25** CENTS

Cover star. By 1959, Hoffa was notorious. His mob links were an open secret: this Life cover promises to expose the "Sources of a Union's Uncurbed Power."

goods until they'd won a better deal from their employers. It was just the beginning.

In the early 1930s, Hoffa became a member of the International Brotherhood of Teamsters, rising fast to become president of the Detroit chapter. The Teamsters were one of the most powerful unions in the United States—they controlled the transport of goods countrywide, and could paralyze a city or district with almost immediate effect simply by withdrawing their services. Ambitious, energetic, and a naturally aggressive negotiator, Hoffa had found his métier and rose quickly: By 1952 he was vice president of the union and in 1957 he achieved his ultimate ambition when Dave Beck, the president, was indicted for tax evasion, and, after a long struggle between the two men, Hoffa replaced him.

UNION MAN

It was an era when the unions were riddled with corruption, and the close links between the Teamsters and organized crime were an open secret. Anyone at the top needed to be able to juggle numerous relationships and interests. Over the next ten years, Hoffa played the game with skill and dedication—even his wife admitted that the Teamsters came first with him, ahead of his family and certainly ahead of the law. He was a strong leader; he could deal with Mafia connections and turn them to the Teamsters' advantage. He succeeded in pulling the disparate branches of the union together and implementing a collective bargaining agreement by 1964, too, but he was running out of ways to evade the constant efforts of both the FBI and the then-Attorney General, Robert Kennedy, to reduce his power. Kennedy loathed Hoffa, claiming that he headed "a conspiracy of evil"; on his part Hoffa derided Kennedy as "that little rich kid." Finally they made a charge stick. In 1964, Hoffa was convicted of witness tampering and misuse of fthe Teamsters' pension fund, and, after losing a series of appeals, in March 1967 he entered the Lewisburg Federal Penitentiary to begin a thirteen-year sentence.

His replacement, Frank Fitzsimmons, wasn't such a strong figurehead and both the Mafia and the internal forces in the union found him easier to manipulate; while Hoffa had excelled at holding things together, under Fitzsimmons all kinds of different factions and stresses began to emerge. So when Hoffa cut a deal with the new United States president, Richard Nixon, and was released from jail in 1971, not everyone was pleased to see him back on the scene. Especially since he immediately began a legal fight to free himself of one of the conditions that Nixon had imposed on his release—a ban from holding any position in the Teamsters

"I've said consistently that no employer ever really accepts a union. They tolerate the unions." —*Jimmy Hoffa*

until 1980 at the earliest. Hoffa was keen to get back to work at the head of his union and he didn't intend to let the president, the legal system, or even the Mafia stop him. It was probably this determination that ultimately decided his fate.

THE END OF THE ROAD

Back to July 1975. At the time of his disappearance, Hoffa was attempting to build bridges with both his "official" contacts and with the Mafia; he knew he would need the support of both if he were ever to regain the top spot in the Teamsters. Notes in his diary confirmed that he was expecting to meet with "Tony Pro" and "Tony Jack" that day: Tony Provenzano, a mob-connected union leader from New Jersey, and Tony Giacolone, a local Mafia boss. On the evening of July 30, when her husband failed to return home, Josephine Hoffa reported her husband missing.

The FBI were quick to knock on the two Tonys' doors, but both denied all knowledge of a meeting, and they had ostentatiously solid alibis—Provenzano had been with union officials in New Jersey; Giacolone was at the Southfield Athletic Club, making sure he was seen by as many people as possible. Hoffa's car was still in the parking lot of the Red Fox, unlocked. Who had taken him, and how had they spirited him away?

On August 1, 1975, a truck driver came forward with new evidence. As he had driven past the restaurant two days earlier, a maroon-colored Mercury had pulled out onto the highway so fast that he'd had to swerve to avoid a collision. And he'd noticed Hoffa—a widely recognized local figure—looking out of the rear passenger window. There'd been two men in the front of the car and one more sitting next to Hoffa in the back. It was the only hard piece of news that the case would ever have; after that, the trail didn't so much go cold as split into a thousand pieces.

Listening in. *Hoffa confers with his coaccused, surveillance expert Bernard Spindel, during a court hearing in 1957 in which the pair were defending themselves against a charge of illegal wiretapping.*

THE AFTERMATH

Was the Red Fox parking lot just a transfer point, and had Hoffa expected the meeting to take place elsewhere? One small detail seemed to point that way: The Red Fox was relatively formal and diners were required to wear a jacket and tie. July 30 was a boiling day—the thermometer hit 92 degrees F/33 degrees C—and Hoffa had left home in just a sport shirt and slacks. And there was someone well-known to Hoffa who drove a maroon Mercury: Charles O'Brien. Known as

Declarations of guilt

Quite a few people have confessed to having killed Jimmy Hoffa. None of the confessions quite add up, though it began to seem that no mob memoir was complete without an admission of guilt. The two the FBI deemed most likely were Frank Sheeran, a known contract killer, who claimed to have murdered Hoffa in a deathbed memoir in 2003, and Richard Kuklinski, "The Iceman," who died in 2005 shortly after a prison confession to his lawyer. Kuklinski said that he had driven Hoffa's body to a scrapyard: "He's part of a car somewhere in Japan right now."

Scene of a murder? *The Red Fox Inn. Hoffa was spirited away from its parking lot—but the FBI concluded that he was probably alive when he left.*

Chuckie, O'Brien had been treated by Hoffa almost as a surrogate son—he was friendly with Hoffa's family and was in and out of his home regularly; Hoffa would have trusted him enough to have accepted a ride. He told police that Hoffa had never been in his car, though, and denied being anywhere in the vicinity of the restaurant—in fact, O'Brien claimed that he hadn't seen his mentor for three weeks, and he certainly took pains to avoid Hoffa's family in the wake of the disappearance. Twenty-six years later he would be proved to have lied on one point at least: DNA tests on hair found in the Mercury established that Hoffa had been in the car, although not when.

In 1975, however, DNA work was still in its infancy. And, whether or not Hoffa had been in O'Brien's car, the trail had gone cold. The FBI were left to follow up on leads offered by informers, and have only ever made some of them public, despite numerous pleas by Hoffa's family. Forty years on, an estimated dozen searches in a wide variety of locations have clocked up a bill of more than $3 million dollars, and resulted in more than sixteen thousand legally logged pages on the case. In 1982, after the statutory seven-year wait, Hoffa was declared legally dead, but interest remains unabated, and the disappearance has sparked a small industry of its own. Literally dozens of books have been published, their contents ranging from conspiracy theory to gangland confessional, every one of which claims to know what really happened—and the whereabouts of Hoffa's remains.

WHERE'S THE BODY?

By October 1975, the FBI were making a fingertip search of the contents of a trash compactor at the Raleigh House Restaurant, 5 miles/8 kilometers up the road from the Red Fox. Tipped off by a source that Hoffa's body had been concealed in a garbage truck and hauled off to the site, they found nothing. In December, a new search started, this time in a vast landfill site in Jersey City. This one was the result of a tip that claimed Hoffa had been strangled, then loaded into a 55-gallon/200-liter oil drum and dumped there. Again, nothing was found.

Over time claims for where the body might be became more exotic. One of the most elaborate was made by a convicted Mafia enforcer, Donald Frankos ("Tony the Greek" to his mob connections), through the odd medium of an interview with *Playboy* magazine. He claimed that Chuckie O'Brien had brought Hoffa to a private house in the city of Mount Clemens, where another mob connection, Jimmy Coonan, had shot him, then cut his body into pieces and buried it under Section 107 of the New York Giants' stadium in New Jersey. In 2010, a TV program went on a mission to dig before the stadium was demolished—but, again, found nothing.

One of the stories the FBI found more likely came from Frank Sheeran, a Pennsylvania Teamsters official and old friend of Hoffa. He confessed to his biographer that he had lured Hoffa to a private house in suburban Detroit on the orders of Russell Bufalino, yet another Mafia boss, where he shot him, dismembered the body and burned the remains in the incinerator in a nearby funeral home whose owner had mob connections. This one sparked enough interest for the authorities to track down the house in 2004, the year after Sheeran's death. They searched it thoroughly and found bloodstains on the floorboards—but they weren't a match with Hoffa's DNA.

And so it went on. In 2006, the search of a farm, specifically the site of an old horse barn, about 30 miles/50 kilometers from the Red Fox, clocked up $250,000, with the involvement of a number of forensics experts alongside heavy digging equipment. Result: nada. In 2012, the poured-cement driveway of a private house in Roseville, a Detroit suburb, was excavated; the home had belonged to one of Tony Giacolone's men and neighbors remembered cement mixing going on at some very odd hours around the time of Hoffa's disappearance. Nothing was found. The most bizarre claim of all was made by Hoffa's colleague Joe Franco, who claimed that the FBI themselves had taken him up in a private airplane—and pushed him out over Lake Michigan. The most recent search took place in 2013, and the myths and tips show no signs of drying up.

Like father, like son. Hoffa with his son, James Junior, admiring the menu for a testimonial dinner held in Hoffa Senior's honor.

THE INHERITANCE

And what of the people left behind? Josephine died of cancer in 1980, five years after her husband disappeared. Hoffa's children have endured an adulthood shadowed by the fate of their father. In the 1990s, in an interview with the *Washington Post*, Barbara claimed to have had a vision of Jimmy Hoffa on the day that he disappeared, and to have known instantly that he was dead. Today, she is a retired judge living in Missouri. Asked if she was ashamed of anything her father did, her reply was trenchant: "I was never embarrassed by my father. Not one day of my life. Never ever."

James P. Hoffa Junior trained as a lawyer and used his heritage to climb to the top of the tree, becoming General President of Teamsters himself in 1999. He has subsequently been reelected three times running, and is currently serving his fourth term. He's at pains to stress that the union's mob links are in the past; in one election speech, he claimed: "The mob killed my father. If you vote for me, they will never come back."

The case of their father's abduction and murder remains open.

> "I was never embarrassed by my father. Not one day of my life. Never ever." —*Barbara Hoffa*

INDEX

IMAGE CREDITS